Design: A Business Case

Design: A Business Case

Thinking, Leading, and Managing by Design

Brigitte Borja de Mozota
Steinar Valade-Amland

Illustrations: Morten U. Petersen, Reflekt Design, Copenhagen

Design: A Business Case: Thinking, Leading, and Managing by Design

First published in 2020 by
Business Expert Press, LLC
222 East 46th Street, New York, NY 10017
www.businessexpertpress.com

First Indian Edition published in 2021 by
Mugdha Misri Chakravartty for BluOne India LLP
306, Tower -I, Assotech Business Cresterra,
Plot no. 22, Sector 135, Noida, India.
Website: www.bluone.ink
Email: publisher@bluone.ink

ISBN: 978-81-949547-4-3

Business Expert Press Portfolio and Project Management Collection
Collection ISSN: 2156-8189 (print)
Collection ISSN: 2156-8200 (electronic)

Interior design by S4Carlisle Publishing Services Private Ltd.,
Chennai, India

Printed in India at Thomson Press (India) Ltd.

Abstract

This book argues the business case for design excellence in organization – whether your mission is to develop new products, services, or procedures or to change existing ones into something better. Although design thinking has reigned for some years now, design management has been left in the shadows. However, design thinking without design making – *skillfully integrated and properly managed* – easily becomes hollow and meaningless. Design excellence requires knowledge, as well as end-to-end management, of the resources and the creative energy that go into development and change processes. Design thinking – made up of the acknowledgment of design skills, of methodological choices, the right mindset, and a conducive culture – is dynamic and adaptable to the project itself and the people involved. Design thinking is a framework developed to ensure C-suite endorsement, strategic coherence, stakeholder engagement, and design excellence in all actions undertaken by the organization. Design management is a rigorous and strategically anchored mechanism to capitalize on the investment in design as intellectual capital. And design – as we've always known it – is the skills and methods and creative capabilities needed to embody ideas and direction. Design thinking inspires, design management enables, design embodies. Only when the three play together as a team, the result is design excellence. *Design: A Business Case* challenges you to stimulate innovation in your own organization, to make design a dialogue between complementary skills, to see design as a bridge between mind and matter, image and identity.

Keywords

design; design management; design thinking; business thinking; organizational design; management; leadership; excellence; design leadership

Contents

Foreword

When I was admitted into The Royal Danish Academy of Fine Arts Schools of Architecture, Design and Conservation in 2008, one of my main areas of study and interest was "web design" and "multimedia design." Fast-forward a little over a decade and these fields of design have "disappeared" and developed into a much richer, sophisticated world of User Experience Design, where designers today may identify themselves as interaction designers, visual designers, information architects, UX strategists, etc. Looking back even further, beyond my own career in design, you'll find a fascinating evolution of the craft of designing objects and buildings into a practice with a plethora of specializations going well beyond our initial definitions of the profession. Design is no longer necessarily manifested by a physical artefact but can be a process, a way of thinking, speculation, or a critical comment. This evolution has started positioning design not only as a craft, but also as a general approach to problem solving, valuable for not only design practitioners, but any individual navigating today's complexity. This has democratized the value of design but has also started a valuable discourse on what aspects of designing can truly be owned and attributed to designers. However, it has also created confusion about what designers are and what they do.

One might ask, if everything is design, then what is a designer? As a practitioner myself, this is a question I'm asked a lot and from time to time, admittedly, ask myself.

New approaches to design coexist with traditional ones. Rather than focusing on the latest trends in design, this book attempts to provide a useful lay of the land while bridging it with similar and complementary concepts in business, strategy, and management. As design's impact expands, the need for contextualizing it with other disciplines increases. This highlights not only how some of the core concepts of design do not exist in a silo, but equips anybody with a design mindset with the vocabulary to bridge their activities and thinking into other disciplines, breaking down barriers and enabling innovation and collaboration across the board. The book provides a comprehensive overview of design's evolution from a differentiator to a transformator to what to many companies today is an integral part of their business and a contributor to good business.

I first became acquainted with the work of Steinar Valade-Amland when he served as the CEO of Danish Designers in 2010. During this time, the Danish School of Design was undergoing its transition to university status while merging with The Royal Danish Academy of Fine Arts, which led us to a number of discussions on the future of the design profession, and, in particular, design education. The authors of this book, Brigitte Borja de Mozota and Steinar Valade-Amland, combine their unique perspectives from consulting, academia, and industry to provide a much needed overview and state of the art of design.

This book serves as a good refresher for any design professional but also as a great introduction for anybody with a design curiosity – about the past, present, and also future of design in the face of new global challenges.

Philip Battin
Head of Seed Studio at Google

Introduction

Design: A Business Case challenges you to stimulate innovation in your own organization, to make design a dialogue between complementary skills, to see design as a bridge between mind and matter, image and identity.

How a Global Crisis Released a Wealth of Tacit Design Thinking

Although conscious of the need to tread carefully, not to be accused of profiteering on the crisis that the world found itself in earlier this year, and for which we will all have to change our outlook for the near and distant future, we cannot but share a few observations we've made in the last six months. One of the most encouraging was how agile and adaptable thousands of companies around the world proved in response to the situation. The COVID-19 crisis has evidenced how design activity flourishes – on at least three different levels – when extreme disruption of "business as usual," external constraints, and sudden, dire needs drive innovation.

Influencing outputs. Coming from high-tech as well as traditional manufacturing industries, companies – multinationals and SMEs alike, as well as individual professionals from design and engineering, business and the arts – took on the challenge of addressing and giving tangible answers to a series of unarticulated yet universally understood briefs. They developed new products, new production lines, new assembly methods – even new materials – to serve a global market in need of protective gear, respiratory products, and other items of which the world experienced a sudden and life-threatening shortage but, clearly, also to survive a situation where traditional markets collapsed and supply chain vanished. Such adaptiveness and agility have never been seen before, and it only proves what an untapped potential for design thinking and design actually exists out there.

Influencing organizations and institutions. At the same time, we've seen a mind-blowing civic engagement and creativity. New grassroots movements have emerged, developed services, established distribution channels, and filled unmet needs, mostly on a voluntary basis, but still a manifestation of the spare capacity out there. And for those who were lucky enough to hold on to their jobs, new ways of working grew out of needs and accumulated, however often mostly through trial and error, experience; ways that overnight became the rule rather than the exception. Never before have digital capabilities been boosted as fast and as effectively among baseline users as during spring 2020.

Influencing frameworks. Perhaps less overt, and yet possibly with a more significant and also more lasting effect, are some of the discourses emerging in the wake of the crisis. People are starting to question whether capitalism as we know it needs reinventing and whether the values and structures on which we build our societies are resilient enough to withstand crises of such a magnitude. Questions also include whether new forms of leadership are needed; more systemic and more collaborative narratives – across borders and in recognition of the mutual dependence that globalization imposes on us. In the aftermath of crises, great visions are born, new stories and new identities.

All this tells us that disruption and despair are catalysts for creativity and hidden talents. It also tells us that lateral thinking has become a premise, rather than frosting on the cake.

> *The design process is a convenient format for developing the idea of lateral thinking. The emphasis is on the different ways of doing things, the different ways of looking at things and the escape from cliché concepts, the challenging of assumptions.*[1]

Never before were challenging assumptions more appropriate, more important. And never before did design capture as many agendas simultaneously.

---

[1]E. de Bono. 1970. *Lateral Thinking – A textbook of Creativity* (London, UK: Penguin Books).

Design as a Bridge between Mind and Matter, Image and Identity

Bridging design and business is a challenge that calls for the courage to transcend a series of stereotypes and to fight against numerous and often extremely well-built silos. It requires that bridges are built between the silos of academic research and the silos of consultancy, between different takes on management and between different takes on design, as well as between the many silos surrounding design management research. And, not least, between the ignorant and the informed, of the value of design. Building bridges is the main objective of *Design: A Business Case*.

It is a conversation and a project, codesigned by two individuals, one from academia and the other from the world of business consultancy and organizational development. We have both – for give or take 30 years – engaged in building theoretical knowledge and empirical evidence on the subject of design in business. From time to time, we met in European and international design meetings, often invited as experts, representing our own countries or our own ideas, in parallel with the pursuit of our separate international careers, with different tools and with different mindsets. However, as a pair representing the domains of both business, practice, education, and research, we found ourselves resembling a "T-shaped profile,"[2] being experts in our own domains, while horizontally exploring each other's expertise of and approach to design. This book comes out of a shared vision of creating a better understanding of the common space, existing between design and business, triggered by a series of joint experiences with and reflections about why it has proven so difficult for business and design to build trust in each other.

Design management researchers that publish and deliver conferences both in design and in management circles are very rare. One of this book's authors has done that in an attempt, albeit unsuccessful, to develop an independent and common space for design management research. A fundamental reason for that is the structural organization of academic research. Design management is a topic that interests researchers in both

[2]M.T. Hansen. 2010. Chief Executive: *IDEO CEO Tim Brown: T-Shaped Stars: The Backbone of IDEO's Collaborative Culture.*

design and management, but on both sides, they look at it through the lenses of their own individual backgrounds of either design science or business science.

Researchers tend to communicate with other researchers within the same domain; the same professional interest, the same research objective, or the same geographical area, and the homogeneity continues downstream. Design researchers reproduce the silos of design: service design, fashion design, industrial design, graphic design, UX or experience design. That might be one of the reasons why the red thread of design science remains invisible to people outside of the design community. When design is portrayed project by project, design management is limited to managing that project better – better processes, better teams, and better performance.

Business researchers reproduce the silos of organizations. They specialize in finances, strategy, human resources, R&D, marketing, supply chain, communications, or any other specific field of business performance. They publish in research journals that replicate exactly the same silos in order to have a career in academia.

This structure does not exactly help to promote trans-, cross-, and interdisciplinarity or to transfer best practices between industries. Because of the structures of academic research, design science is interesting to business scientists only if it fits into existing business concepts and into their field of expertise, such as innovation, organizational creativity, branding, customer behavior or whatever else, and even then, they focus only on the contents in design science that fit into their silos. In this structure of vertical silos with rigorous institutional constraints for researchers – at least if they are career minded – the global picture is missed, and the potential for applying approaches inspired by design remains unexplored. Our objective is to discuss design, design management, and design thinking as part of the big picture, beyond all silos.

Let's admit, though, that the situation has improved a little lately. Business journals are now open to design management as a theme and will even get a dedicated issue of *Journal of Product Innovation Management* in 2020. Design schools, traditionally tending to prefer design professionals as teachers, now open up for PhD researchers and academics from other fields. So there is actually hope that a virtuous circle from research to pedagogy might start both in business and in design education. But still, the role of design in business schools is selective and fragmented and does not contribute to mitigating the cultural difference between the two educational systems. Design might be mentioned in some courses – entrepreneurship, innovation, and marketing – but still rarely in key management subjects like performance, finances, operations, or knowledge management.

Finally, we also recognize the silos of the "convinced." Design management thrives in silos consisting of companies convinced of the value of design, benchmarking between themselves, in networks such as national design promotion centers and the Design Management Institute, celebrating each other at conferences and awards ceremonies. The same companies are quoted again and again, which might limit the interest for design to the business community at large.

A Shared Vision of Design as Business Performance

By sharing information originating in all the aforementioned silos, we hope that a vision of design for business will emerge and be shared, a vision that would foster an understanding of why design – why giving form to societal interfaces – is an economic, managerial, political, and financial act that fits into a multitude of strategic conversations.

Every time designers draw an artefact, they make a statement about the direction the world ought to take. It is now admitted that the design profession contributes to the success of national economies on many levels: reputation, creative industries, intellectual property, innovation, exports, and revitalization of territories, just as much as there is a correlation between design and company performance and strategy, and just as the economic competitiveness of a country is measured by its capacity to innovate and to undertake research. The next step will be to embrace design, design management, and design thinking in the quest to meet the needs of tomorrow, not only our own needs for material and immaterial well-being, but also the needs of future generations. Design is no longer a sectorial craft, nor is it merely a matter of competitive advantage and differentiation, and no longer – if it ever were – a boardroom issue.

Design: A Business Case challenges you to stimulate innovation in your own organization; to make design a dialogue between complementary skills; and to see design as a bridge between mind and matter, image and identity. It is conceived not only as a business case for design, but, equally, as an appeal to use design as a business case format for all the other ventures, changes, and challenges you – as a business leader – stand face to face with.

PART 1

An untapped potential lies in bridging design – as a skill, a mindset, and a methodology – to the most dominant agendas of business literature and business thinking: innovation and resilience, organizational change and experience, and strategic direction and management.

What Is Design Management?

Whereas some things change gradually and almost inconspicuously over time, other things change abruptly and often with big waves, uncertainty, and disbelief following in their wake. Design belongs to both categories. On the one hand, its role has changed gradually, responding to the continuous changes in economics and society at large. As only one example, the rise of service industries gradually brought about the concept of service design, as did austerity in the public sector. The rise of the digital economy brought with it UX design and interaction design, and the quest for new mechanisms to deal with increased complexity across sectors paved the way for the rise of design thinking.

On the other hand, albeit often disconnected from current design practice, design has captured the interest of business media and political agendas, new design disciplines have emerged, new evidence has disrupted the discourse, and new case studies of what has come out of design processes have been published, tending to progress the way that design is perceived and talked about in leaps and lapses. One strand of design still comes from the applied arts, applying free creativity to explore and make tangible how the world could be. This so-called research practice of design is often seen in luxury, fashion, and home decoration sponsored by design editors. Then there is mainstream design, answering business brief – and there are the critics of such practice, often encountered in design education and theory. Thus, design follows the waves, but also contests and fights them by offering alternative concepts to mainstream perceptions of meaning and value. Now, when the wicked problems of society change, the scope of design changes accordingly. But design has too often been referred to merely as an embodiment of an artefact or environment conceived in someone's creative mind. One of the front-runners in articulating the role of design was Victor Papanek, who wrote thirty years ago that

> *Design must become an innovative, highly creative, cross-disciplinary tool responsive to the true needs of men.*

and

> *The ultimate job of design is to transform man's environment and tools and, by extension, man himself.*[1]

Despite some pioneer directors of companies, or even heads of state, who understood the role of design in business, like the Duke of Weimar, who as early as 1902 employed the architect Henry van de Velde to drive the region's crafts and industries through design, or pioneers in the British arts and crafts movement and directors of companies like Wedgwood or W. Morris and later the German company AEG with Peter Behrens, design started taking on different meanings and uses decade by decade up through the second half of the twentieth century, and even more rapidly since then. These were some of the first examples of design strategy.

Anna Valtonen[2] captured this development in a very structured and accessible manner but focused on in-house design activities in Finland, but the overall picture painted easily translates into a more general picture of the perception of design in the industrialized parts of the world.

---

[1]V. Papanek. 1984. *Design for the Real World: Human Ecology and Social Change* (London: Thames & Hudson).

[2]A. Valtonen. 2005. *Six Decades – and Six Different Roles for the Industrial Designer* [Nordes Conference in the Making]. Copenhagen; May 30-31, 2005.

Although design existed long before the fifties – Bauhaus more than justifies that claim – designer as a professional role and identity emerged in the late forties and was consolidated in the fifties. Back then, design focused on taking the decorative arts, crafts, and industrial traditions one step further by adding new aesthetic trends and languages, new material innovations, new cross-disciplinary methods, and physical representations of national identity primarily to furniture and other home products. In the sixties, design moved from the wood and metal shops and creative studies of what we today know as design icons to the development environments in other industries: from typewriters to telephones and measuring devices and pumps, yet still being applied to physical products and, to a certain extent, also to visual identities, marketing collaterals, and packaging.

The Three Phases of Design and Design Management

First Phase of Design and Design Management: 1975 to 1993

In the seventies, design research emerged, often referred to as design studies. These studies of design issues scrutinized the impact that design had on industrial value creation as well as the perceived values of the users of designed objects, as opposed to objects that had not undergone an actual design process, as measured by both ergonomic and emotional experiences. In parallel with research gaining momentum, governments introduced various forms of design promotion and design support policies and initiatives. Hence, the economic impacts of design were slowly recorded and documented – pioneered by the design management movement in the U.S., Design Management Institute (DMI), and its sister movements in Europe. Design management slowly emerged as key to managing the relationship between a design consultancy and its client[3] and as a more robust platform for discussing design as a significant factor for growth and competitiveness.

Then, in the eighties, design management captured the attention of larger companies in particular, acknowledging the reflections of Philip Kotler in an article from 1984, where he asserts that "each company has

[3]M. Farr. 1966. *Design Management* (London: Hodder and Stoughton).

to decide on how to incorporate design into the marketing planning process."[4] A key factor was the growing corporate focus on competitive advantage through brand management, which also resonated well with the brand orientation of design management.

Second Phase of Design and Design Management: 1993 to 2005

This period saw the start of academic research on design management, driven, among others, by DMI, and the worldwide launch of master programs and syllabus on design management. This new, more comprehensive and encompassing role of design, supported by a previously unmatched academic interest in design and design management, changed not only the way in which design was perceived, but also where in the organization its value was recognized.

This ascent through the hierarchies continued in the nineties, where design as a differentiator – as a brand carrier – dominated the design discourse, while it slowly gathered momentum also among policy makers in the first decade of the 21st century – as its focus on innovation suddenly converged with ongoing discussions on how to improve competitiveness and resilience in an increasingly globalized and competitive marketplace. The economic effect of design was tested and evidenced, such as in the Danish Design Centre's surveys from 2003, repeated and validated in 2008,[5] measuring design activity versus company performance in more than a thousand companies. In parallel, the idea of a learning curve of design management through the "Design Ladder" model, introduced by Danish Design Centre[6] emerged, based on statistics of design integration in companies according to their level of understanding: design as style, as a process, as strategy, or as culture (Figure 1).

---

[4]P. Kotler and G.A. Rath. 1984. "Design: A Powerful but Neglected Strategic Tool," *Journal of Business Strategy* 5, no. 2, pp. 16-21.

[5]National Agency for Enterprise and Housing. 2003/2008. *The Economic Effects of Design, Design skaber værdi – udbredelse og effekter af design (Design Creates Value – spread and effects of design)* (Copenhagen: National Agency for Enterprise and Housing).

[6]Danish Design Centre. 2015. *The Design Ladder: Four Steps of Design Use* (Copenhagen: Danish Design Centre).

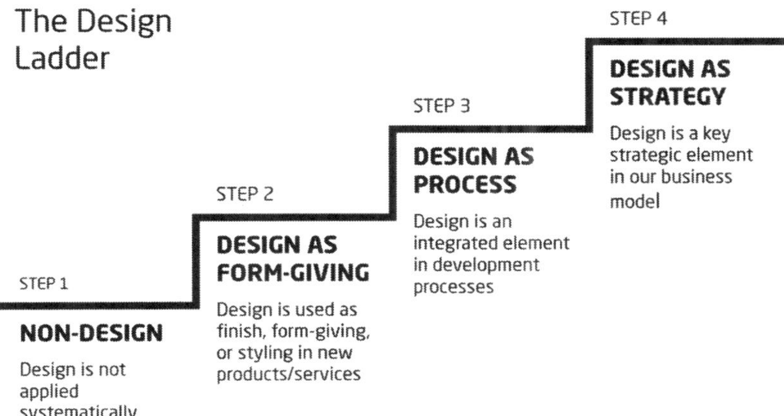

Figure 1 The Design Ladder: Four Steps of Design Use

This was the first time a study was done with the CEOs of design-oriented European SMEs, asking their opinions about design value, using 20 variables from previously documented design research. This research was built using Michael Porter's value chain[7] as a framework. The results were eye-opening, because there was no single vision of design management and design value, while the replies clustered in three groups. In her European research published in 2002 and 2006, one of the authors of this book, Brigitte Borja de Mozota, proposes the model Designence, which gives a strategic view of design value (Figure 2). This model was further turned into an operational tool for designers and designer managers using the Balanced Scorecard model, "The Four Powers of Design."[8]

---

[7]M.E. Porter. 1985. *Competitive Advantage* (New York, NY: The Free Press), Ch. 1, pp. 11-15.

[8]B.Borja de Mozota. 2002 – reprint in 2006. "The Four Powers of Design: A Value Model in Design Management," *Design Management Review* 17, no. 2. Reprint 2011 Handbook on Design Management Research (Berg) after 2006.

Figure 2 The Designence model: "The Four Powers of Design – a Value Model in Design Management"

Third Phase of Design and Design Management: From 2005 Until Today

A game changer in the perception of design value was Hertenstein, Platt, and Veryzer's article on design management in 2005.[9] This was the first time that the role of design – not only as a brand asset, but also as an evidenced source of user-centered innovation capacity – was scientifically demonstrated. Development of design management awards in Europe and the U.S. started showing how good design management works in competitive real-life contexts, emphasizing how improvement processes were approached through design-driven innovation. Slowly, another layer was added, as testimonials of the capability of design to influence corporate culture strategically emerged. As present times are all about reinventing

---

[9]J.H. Hertenstein, M.B. Platt, and R.W. Veryzer. 2005. "The Impact of Industrial Design Effectiveness on Corporate Financial Performance," *Journal of Product Innovation Management* 22, pp. 3–21.

organizations and institutions toward more human ways of doing business, the importance of giving more power and initiative to designers in order to foster transformation currently defines the design management discourse, possibly because it has proven to be as valid for entrepreneurs and digital "start-ups" as for traditional industries (Figure 3).

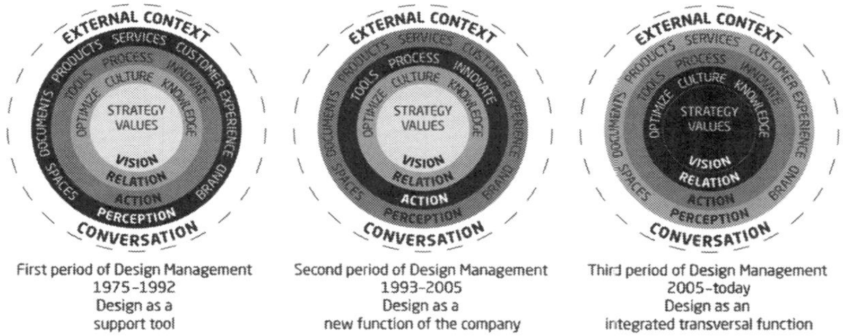

Figure 3 Forty years of design management research: a litterature study and the paths for the future

Source: Brigitte Borja de Mozota. 2018. "Quarante ans de recherche en design management: une revue de littérature et des pistes pour l'avenir," *Sciences du Design* 1, no. 7, pp. 28-45.

As for the more hands-on approach to design management, recent research supports the assumption that the return on investment from design – conceived, applied, and managed professionally – is significantly higher than that of organizations that employ design randomly and without strategic intent: "Companies that manage design effectively and efficiently attain better product innovation performance than those that do not."[10] These assumptions have also been supported by other sources, such as Tom Inns' contribution to the report "The Value of Design" from 2014.[11]

In more recent research carried out by Forrester for IBM, projects undertaken with the IBM's Design Thinking Practice showed a return on investment over three years of 301 percent, besides slashing the

[10]A. Fernández-Mesa, J. Alegre, R. Chiva-Gómez and A. Gutiérrez-Gracia. 2012. *Design Management Capability: Its Mediating Role Between Organizational Learning Capability and Innovation Performance in SMEs. DRUID Academy 2012 (University of Cambridge/The Moeller Centre)*

[11]Arts and Humanities Research Council (AHRC). 2014. *Expert Workshop Report* (Glasgow: AHRC).

time required for initial design and alignment by 75 percent, reducing development and testing time by 33 percent, cutting design defects by 50 percent, improving product outcomes, reducing the risk of costly failures, and increasing portfolio profitability (Figure 4).[12]

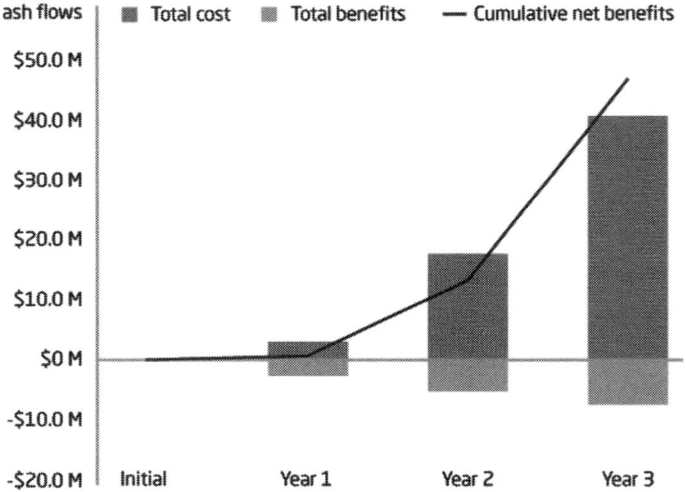

Figure 4 Forrester Consulting (2018): The Total Economic Impact of IBM's Design Thinking Practice

Thus, the case for design as a methodology and approach that has the potential to significantly enhance the competitiveness of commercial suppliers of products and services as well as communication, services, and environments delivered by public service providers has finally been thoroughly and scientifically underpinned.

---

[12]Forrester Consulting. 2018. *The Total Economic Impact™ of IBM's Design Thinking Practice; How IBM Drives Client Value and Measurable Outcomes With Its Design Thinking Framework* (Cambridge, MA: Forrester Consulting).

In order to develop the skills needed for the 21st century – human skills such as empathy, teamwork, innovation, and problem-solving skills – companies are turning toward design thinking methods, introducing them to empathy and user-driven engagement techniques, experimentation, and prototyping – proven valuable, whether for products or services development or for government policies, health care, and public service innovation. What is more interesting, however, is the realization that design in itself has become an instrument for building resilient business cases and resilient organizations. Several recent books deal with the relationship between resilience and stakeholder engagement, prototyping, and exploration – between resilience and design:

> *Resilient organizations are able to address pivotal events that affect their business because they are alert to, and anticipate both internal and environmental changes – opportunities as well as challenges – and effectively respond to those changes using available resources in a timely, flexible, affordable and relevant manner.*[13]

and

> *The most powerful lever for enhancing resilience is design, in the broadest possible sense. The scope of design must expand from products and processes to the enterprise as a whole, exploring how changing external conditions might influence business success. Our recommended approach to 'design for resilience' considers the health and viability of important external systems, including stakeholders, communities, infrastructure, supply chains and natural resources.*[14]

During this journey, in some companies, design became increasingly integrated into corporate strategies and dependent on close

---

[13]L. Holbeche. 2015. *The Agile Organization: How to Build an Innovative, Sustainable and Resilient Business* (London: Kogan Page).

[14]J. Fiksel. 2015. *Resilient by Design: Creating Businesses That Adapt and Flourish in a Changing World* (Washington, DC: Island Press).

collaboration between those who trained to become designers and others who played increasingly important roles in the design process. This increased complexity called for a certain mode of management, and design management organically grew into a professional métier in its own right. Since its emergence in the 1960s, design management has grown and matured into a globally recognized industry. It started out as a process and methodology for managing creative projects through an organization – most often a linear process following standard project management taxonomies. However, while design management was used as a means of managing creative processes from its inception, a more recent approach to design management is to consider it as a means of enhancing the ability of an organization to take up new knowledge and embrace creativity on a strategic level and as an integrated element of organizational or corporate culture, revealing its commonalities with concepts like design thinking and the emerging discipline of organizational design. And yet however established design research and the measurement of design effectiveness has become as an academic discipline and domain, after four decades of struggling to be embraced by the business community, it is surprising how many executives with R&D, services, or business development responsibility are utterly unfamiliar with the concept. A report published by Lancaster University states that

> *Despite the recognition of the value of design and its importance for innovation, companies found it very difficult to measure the return of investments made on design. This difficulty of putting a monetary value to the impact produced by design is partly due to conceptual and practical problem of separating design from other activities contributing to innovation.*[15]

[15] R. Cooper, R.J. Hernandez, E. Murphy and B. Tether. 2016. *Design Value: The Role of Innovation in Design* (Lancaster: Lancaster University).

An untapped potential, however, lies in bridging design – as a skill, a mindset, and a methodology – with the most dominant agendas of business literature and business thinking:

- innovation and resilience
- organizational change and experience
- strategic direction and management

This potential can be exploited only by linking the changes in the contexts, environments, and challenges of the 21st century to designers' capabilities, design, and design value. In response to that, some of the leading representative bodies of design and designers quite recently issued a joint declaration of what design is:

> *Design is the application of intent: the process through which we create the material, spatial, visual and experiential environments in a world made ever more malleable by advances in technology and materials, and increasingly vulnerable to the effects of unleashed global development.*[16]

Exploring this new approach to design as an integrated business case instrument – rather than further exploring the business case of using design as an add-on – is driven by an ambition to demonstrate how design thinking and design management equal design excellence. Design excellence enhances the most cited management gurus' thinking by adding a new layer of framing problems, enhancing ideation and adding a tangible dimension to strategic development, innovation, and organizational change. Our objective is neither to challenge nor to profiteer from the existing valuable and firmly entrenched insights to which most companies and organizations around the world – directly or indirectly and knowingly or unknowingly – could probably and rightly attribute their success. Merely to inspire another perspective on those, already widespread insights.

[16] *Montréal Design Declaration* – issued at the 2017 World Design Summit.

PART 2

Just as there is a need for more understanding of business among designers and a better understanding of what design is and what it can do among business people, there is also a need for a more profound understanding in many businesses of what they want to achieve and what can help them achieve it.

Why Design Management Now?

We have set out to explore

Why Companies Are Not Using Design Strategically Despite Decades of Studies and Evidence

As part of that exploration, we need to explore where the fears of using design come from and discuss what went wrong in the pursuit of creating an understanding of what design, design thinking, and design management can do. Although the fear of engaging strategically with design and designers exists, we also believe that, as with most other fears, it is based on a combination of biases, experience, and facts. Thus, as facing one's fears is a first step to new discoveries, we will suggest some of the reasons for this fear and, hopefully, help those who recognize it in themselves to challenge the biases, revisit their experiences, and discuss how the facts can be overcome. We therefore start with four theses for why these gaps are still there.

What the Most Imminent Challenges of Management Are

We also need to explore the major challenges of management to find out how design, design thinking, and design management could better resonate with the needs in organizations under constant pressure of improved performance. As part of this exploration, we will later present a case study on how a public sector design and innovation unit has harvested the success of working systematically with design excellence, and thus also, albeit indirectly, the community that it serves.

What Happens When Design Thinking and Design Management Are Added to Strategy

A healthier equilibrium between design thinking and design management is needed. We need to show the different roles they play but, not least, to demonstrate the immense potential represented by applying both – side by side and in sequence, adding up to design excellence – to manage change and to counter the fear that change tends to carry with it. Design thinking is an invaluable source of insight and inspiration, whereas design management is an equally valuable key to enabling great solutions. Design thinking inspires and informs, and by reflecting the vision of an organization's leadership, it empowers the organization to pursue and persevere. Design management enables by putting in place the knowledge, structures, and resources necessary to transform a vision into tangible results, to embody its creative capital through design.

Despite a rather massive pool of documentation accumulated over the last two decades, demonstrating the effectiveness of design has proven difficult, whether applied to specific sectors or, at large, to small and medium enterprises (SMEs) in particular or the public sector. It is all there and, on a general note, quite convincing. And yet the growth in the number of organizations working strategically with design is hardly growing. This, of course, leads to asking what makes design so different from other concepts and approaches introduced during the same window of time – with far greater success in terms of penetration – concepts like lean and agile, just to mention two. We will try to discuss some possible causes and effects.

Four Theses on Design's Unsuccessful Penetration

Thesis # 1.

Q: Why are so few using design strategically despite design's overwhelming case?

A: Perhaps we need to revisit the discussion about what design is...

Unfortunately, history shows that the design community waited very long before it started taking its own medicine: starting with understanding the user. The discourse and the cases and all the storytelling around it – what design was and was coming to – revolved around the design industry itself. A more end-user-centric approach to arguing the role and value of design has emerged much more recently, but we still see remains of designer-centric design – in fact, popular media seem to find this kind of design much more interesting than designs that actually make a difference to someone who is not a design aficionado. One could suggest that designers are so sure of their own worth – of their talent to create value and of the inherent qualities of their professions – that they forgot to ask basic questions about their market: who they were and what they needed. Big parts of the design community failed to understand and accept that people at large did not truly understand what the hype was all about. And how could anyone expect the marketplace to demand design services when they had a hard time understanding what design was all about?

Design management supported by the adoption of a design research attitude has provided help and guidance to overcome this barrier for decades through a vocabulary and a logic that did not originate in the design community. They aimed at explaining in understandable ways what the methods and principles of design were, the nature of and skills needed to provide professional design services, and what expectations any given company could realistically have from entering into a design process partnership. Unfortunately, this help was never truly embraced by the community of design practitioners and design critics, who hardheadedly continued to discuss design on their own terms and within the confines of the "black box" of design creativity. In consequence, there still tend to be some massive barriers to the understanding of design by nondesigners.

The Ambidexterity and Ambiguity of Design

A starting point for a meaningful discussion about why design is still struggling to be understood could be the many different ways in which design has been portrayed over the last many years. According to Don Norman, Director of The Design Lab at the University of California in San Diego, and a prominent voice in the design debate, it has come to a point where a choice has to be made. In an article in 2017, he says that

> *The move from craft-based to evidence-based design, from simple objects to complex sociotechnical systems, and from craftspeople to design thinkers suggest that we are now faced with a fork in the road with two different possible futures for design: 1) A craft and practice; 2) A mode of thinking.*[1]

He may be right, but there is also the possibility that design might survive and grow with, and is actually fueled by, its own ambiguity. This ambiguity, by the way, in many ways mirrors the thinking around ambidextrous leadership, balancing exploration and exploitation – characterized by many as a key organizational behavior to foster innovation.

> *The concept of ambidexterity informs us that leaders need to develop a broad set of leadership tactics to enable the dualities of innovation captured by terms such as creation and implementation. As the process of innovation unfolds, the importance of each side of a duality, and the set of leader behaviors that are effective, alternate in an iterative manner.*[2]

If we go back to three other prominent design gurus, representing three stages in the development of modern design, they argue three very different but equally important aspects of the design process. Herbert

---

[1]D.A. Norman. 2016. *The Future of Design: When You Come to a Fork in the Road, Take It*, Article Published on May 17, 2016.

[2]R. Bledow, M. Frese and V. Mueller. 2011. "Ambidextrous Leadership for Innovation: The Influence of Culture," *Advances in Global Leadership 6*, pp. 41-69.

Simon represents an approach that could be labeled "problem-solving" – as is clearly discernible in his probably most famous quote from 1969,

> *Everyone designs who devise courses of action aimed at changing existing situations into preferred ones. The intellectual activity that produces material artefacts is no different fundamentally from the one that prescribes remedies for a sick patient or the one that devises a new sales plan for a company or a social welfare policy for a state.*[3]

Moving 15 years ahead, the philosopher Donald Schön introduced an approach to what the core of the design process is, which – to some degree in opposition to Simon – could be labeled as "experimentation." In a book in 1983, he refers to design practice as an exploratory process:

> *When the practitioner reflects in action in a case he perceives as unique, paying attention to phenomena and surfacing his intuitive understanding of them, his experimenting is at once exploratory, move testing and hypothesis testing. The three functions are fulfilled by the very same actions.*[4]

A third, more recent voice in the discourse, Willemien Visser, a cognitive psychologist, reverts to what may seem a rather purist approach to what design is and what could be labeled as "representation." In an article in 2006, she challenges both Simon and Schön:

> *Rather than conceiving designing as problem solving - Simon's symbolic information processing (SIP) approach - or as a reflective practice or some other form of situated activity - the situativity (SIT) approach - we consider that, from a cognitive viewpoint, designing is most appropriately characterised as a construction of representations.*[5]

---

[3]H.A. Simon. 1969. *The Sciences of the Artificial* (Cambridge, MA: MIT Press), 3rd edition 1996.

[4]D.A. Schön. 1983. *The Reflective Practitioner: How Professionals Think in Action* (New York, NY: Basic Books).

[5]W. Visser. 2006. "Designing as Construction of Representations: A Dynamic Viewpoint in Cognitive Design Research," *Human–Computer Interaction* 21, no. 1.

These three approaches currently coexist in some kind of harmony – perhaps in part because they have all challenged the time in which they emerged. Looking back at a less theoretical and rather schematic account of how design was progressively perceived throughout the time span of the three aforementioned researchers' contributions, design started as a representation and a craft, while exploration and experimentation, on the one hand, and problem-solving, on the other, evolved in parallel with the complexity of the problems to be solved and the new ideas to be explored. In a discussion with Fred Collopy[6] a decade or so ago, he framed the act of designing in a fascinating way, saying that *to design is to approach a problem with true concern for all stakeholders, making sure that all interests are duly considered.*

Regardless, however, of how valuable the endeavors of scholars to label design practice and its related process over time are, they have also created an abyss of mistrust between design practitioners, on the one hand, who simply exercised their trade and talents and the various players in the marketplace for design services, on the other, who grew increasingly confused about what design could actually do for them. Another source of cross communication is the liberal use of the term "design" itself, currently including an array of activities ranging from giving form to objects to any form of structured, conscious planning of or method for any conceivable undertaking or process, as an input or as an outcome. Another level of confusion, which has grown out of this proliferation of the concept of design, results in mixing design as a phenomenon, the act of designing, and the designer's unique skill set and approach to the two aforementioned. The three concepts need to be described and defined separately for a meaningful discussion to take place.

Although design as a concept has undergone development from primarily representing an expression in the intersection between the aesthetic and the functional to gradually including a prescribed methodological approach to design as a process, the discussion becomes more complicated when attempting to qualify "designing" as a specific competence and, perhaps even more so, the trained design professional as the sole representative of design as a specific skill set and trade.

---

[6]Fred Collopy is professor at Case Western University in Ohio, USA.

Building our rationale on a synthesis of the approaches of the three design gurus, we see the contours of a concept – design – that encompasses a certain approach to problem-solving, includes exploration and experimentation as part of the process and as a means to finding the best possible solution – integrates physical or visual representations of these experiments, which would often be referred to as prototyping. It also entails that design is

- inherently aspirational: driven by the desire to change, undogmatic
- open to discovery and change of direction, and
- sensorial: depending on physical, visual, or psychological interaction with different stakeholders

One of the authors of this book, in an article on design for the triple bottom line, once made an attempt to capture what design is all about – rather than what design is:

> *Design is about attractiveness, sensuality, aesthetics, and functionality, about real people and real problems, about individuals and their encounters with systems, about encouraging responsible behaviour and choices, about challenging our prejudices, about fellowship and ownership, and about expressing identities for individuals, groups of individuals, corporate entities and society at large. It's true; design is all about people, profit and planet.*[7]

From such an interpretation of design, it is evident that the act of designing requires an ability to integrate and exploit the value of as many accessible, specialized competences as possible. Hence, designers have sovereignty neither to the notion of "designing" nor to the concept of "design". However, the designer can and will often play a significant and often clearly defined role in such processes. This role – based on the unique approaches to problem-solving, dialogue, analysis and method, abstraction, and visualization – as well as the ability to shape, which are all part of their training – becomes one of initiating, encouraging, and

---

[7]S. Valade-Amland. 2011. "Design for People, Profit and Planet," *DMI Review*, 22, no. 1.

creating a framework for, and by means of a professional response, facilitating dialogue and reciprocity between other specific competences in order to design, but also, and as importantly, make others design. One of the classic competences, so to speak, of the design professional is to add to the solution a sensuous and aesthetic dimension, to orchestrate the aesthetic relations between an individual and an object or experience. Thus, this aesthetic dimension also needs to be included in the discussion of both design thinking and design management, not as a goal in itself but as an evidenced means to enhance the performance of human beings, the perceived quality of public services, and the user experience of any given transaction, in addition to the competitiveness that aesthetics add in a market consisting of what you might otherwise consider to be comparable products and services.

Disciplines and Attitudes

Designers come in all kinds of shapes and sizes, and, as a professional trade and practice, designers cover an incredible number of sectors and industries. This, one can argue, makes the challenge of finding the right designer for the right job more difficult than ever. At the same time, as individuals and design firms, we see an increasing degree of specialization, which offers at least a certain degree of solace. There is a conception of designers as being more or less unanimously determined to bring to the world another mind-blowing artefact: a chair or a lamp or a frock, thus entering the hall of fame and becoming a household name. Fame might also be a quite common motivation to start design school, and, admittedly, not everyone ever succeeds at giving up that dream for another, more meaningful mission. However, design education today is about much more than giving form and shape to chairs, lamps, and frocks. Current design curricula focus on solving real problems (Simon), on exploring new and better futures (Schön), and on creating better, more meaningful and more sustainable representations of people's dreams and cravings (Visser). All three are pursued – in parallel and with the same determination to make a difference.

As a result of a constantly growing platform of academic design research as well as new generations of faculty, demonstrating an entirely different aspiration for design as a profession and skill set than their predecessors, design education has improved greatly over the last two decades. Improved, as in becoming much more responsive – albeit inherently with a certain delay, because planning and designing educational programs is often a lengthy process – to the needs of the marketplace and vastly more focused on creating synergies between the three pillars. The main challenge, however, is that the marketplace struggles to see and understand this movement and sometimes seems to remain as confused about what design is and what it can do as it always was.

We will return to a more detailed analysis of the kinds of mindsets, skill sets, and tools that are needed to undertake design thinking, design practice, and design management later on in this book. However, it is crucial to understand that design education does not prepare anyone for all these roles, and even within design practice, different skills and different motivations are needed to excel at different types of design practice. Despite certain commonalities in terms of theory and methods, there is a world of difference between working as an author designer – the kind we know from glossy magazines – and being part of a cross-disciplinary team and a complex value chain. The difference in part exists in the extent to which the designer sees him or herself as a problem solver, an explorer, or a materializer.

Furthermore, design education is characterized by strong attitudes, often guiding both curricula and how design is being talked about on a day-to-day basis. Is design primarily a question of creating commercial value, or is its objective to create better communities, to eradicate poverty, or to fight global warming? Those designers, who are good at the first might not necessarily be very useful to pursue the latter. In other words, design schools and the community of professional designers cannot be blamed for making it easy for potential clients to maneuver in and between the different approaches to design and the vast number of designers, who might not always be very articulate about which type of designer they are, what kind of problems they can solve, and which value chains they fit into.

We have established that the constantly increasing range of design disciplines in combination with diverse attitudes and motivations complicate the search for relevant design resources. Two additional factors, which constitute significant barriers, are language and prejudice.

Creative professionals like designers and business professionals struggle to understand each other. They think differently and speak different languages. Not many design practitioners are verbally articulate about what their expertise is and wherein their value proposition lies. Likewise, few business professionals are able to frame their expectations in a manner that resonates with the aspirations of the designer. Owing to this barrier, countless collaborative projects never got started, and probably even more projects fell to the floor as a result of cross communication.

Lack of insight into each other's professional domains and practice keeps prejudice alive, reciprocally. Unfounded assumptions of untamed creativity and hot air, on the one hand, and ruthless exploitation, on the other, do not exactly further the dialogue between the two. Perhaps this can also account for the fact that designers as professional service providers earn on average a mere 63 percent of what other business advisers do and have an income of only 71 percent of the average salary in Europe.[8] This undervaluation of design as a professional service starts as early as in design school, where smart companies and business professionals see design schools as idea boxes and sources of free concepts and ideas – based, of course, on their understanding of design education as being all about creativity.

What Designers Want To Do...

Whereas business strategies are driven by short- or long-term profit, designers rarely see their role as a means to maximize corporate performance. And when they do, they tend to overestimate the potential role of their own contribution to do so. Only rarely do we see true convergence between the articulated motives and perceived realities of the two parties. Observing the obvious fact that some designers do not fit into the following, on a general note, designers are driven by one or several of the following desires:

- create meaningful products and services
- make the world more beautiful

[8]Bureau of European Design Association (BEDA). 2016. *European Survey of Remuneration of Designers* (Brussels: BEDA).

- make people's life easier
- humanize technology and improve user experience
- protect the planet
- eradicate poverty, famine, and disease

What is interesting, however, is that a vast majority of the world's successful businesses owe their success to excellence within one or more of the same objectives. Hence, there is no fundamental conflict of interest between the business and design communities.

Thesis # 2.

Q: Why do business and design not seem to go all that well together?
A: Perhaps we don't know enough about what excellence in management is...

Business and design come from different places, philosophically as well as with regard to what constitutes value and how it is being measured. Design management exists because of this gap and has, as one of its most significant missions, the need to explain and demonstrate the relationship between the two. And yet the gap is still there, and the prejudice and misconceptions are as fervent as ever. It is not only design advocates who for more than half a century failed at drawing a lifelike portrait of what design is, how it creates value, and why it ought to be top of mind for business leaders; equally unsuccessful has been the business community at articulating what excellence in management is and why this search for excellence constitutes a unique opportunity for design and designers' skills to join the movement – with their aspirations of and tangible propositions for how to achieve such excellence.

Design management has acted – to the extent that its outreach has allowed – as a mediator between design and business, between design and management. This juxtaposition – wedged between design, on the one hand, and management, on the other – has over the last three or four decades proven quite effective at building bridges and of creating a certain degree of understanding and respect between the two. This ongoing bridge building, however, has, unfortunately, reached only a very limited flank of the two communities, namely, the most pragmatic and realistic wings of the design community – boasting ambitions beyond the mere artistic – and the wings of the business community that are more progressive and alert to new movements – realizing that competitiveness and innovation cannot be achieved by cutting costs, by robotizing and technological advance, by scale, or by dumping prices only.

Design Historically Lacks Business Orientation

All professions build palisades around themselves to protect their expertise, their lingo, and their culture. The design community is no different, and even within the perimeters of the design community, there are silos and strong mechanisms to perpetuate the barriers referred to previously.

To the extent that there is a defined design community, it consists of four different categories of players: the community of professional design practitioners, design education, design promotional institutions, and design support centers. All of them dispose of various forms of outreach and mechanisms to communicate with audiences outside of the pond, and all of them tend to have different views on and different relations to the business community and other players on the side of the design services market and procurement. What binds them together is the notion that design is the epicenter of all development and change. The design industry, meaning those who offer professional design services to a professional market, often build a wall of inward-looking communication to guard their domain, often celebrating one another by means of design awards and commemorative publications – invariably focusing on the most iconic designers, the stars, and the provocateurs.

Design schools fight for students and for funding and for convincing figures showing their worth as producers of valuable expertise. Their means range from research and academic articles, primarily reaching an audience of peers, to graduate shows and exhibitions and partnerships with the specific private and public sectors within which their students are prepared to play a future role.

Design promotion centers are often wholly or partially financed by local, regional, or national governments to promote the value of design to audiences ranging from professional communities to the public at large, to show best practices, and to cast some light over how constructive dialogue between designers and industry can lead to more attractive and more user-friendly solutions to tangible or intangible challenges.

Design support mechanisms sometimes come as appendices or integrated elements of promotion centers and sometimes as independent bodies with a mandate to support the growth and professionalization of the design industry as a means of fostering innovation and competitiveness. One typical role of design support mechanisms is to act as a mediator between the design community and the marketplace and to support first-time use of design in companies and organizations.

In addition to these four, a number of other players influence the perception of what design is and what it can do, including trade organizations for designers and design companies, media – professional publications, newspapers and glossy magazines, and business book publishers, art museums, and trade shows.

Altogether, the design industry and design as a professional domain are blessed with more focus and attention, but also with more voices telling different stories, than most other professional communities. What it leaves us with, however, is a professional domain with only limited focus on the actual difference that design can make for what's actually in demand: better profitability and effectiveness in businesses, better services and increased efficiency in the public sectors; and more competent, more agile, and more productive organizations across the board.

How Much Do Designers Care about Business?

The very short and not very friendly answer would be "very little." Designers are often dismayed and discouraged that their clients do not understand what design is. However, judging by the amount of focus on design in business newspapers and magazines, in management books, and even at hard-core business events like World Economic Forum, one could claim that at least the business community makes a wholehearted attempt to grow their awareness and understanding of the value of design. The question is rather whether designers make enough of an effort to understand what it is to run a business, to fight for market shares and margins, to reinvent and innovate propositions and business models to constantly stay on top of the competition, and to keep costs at a minimum, all at the same time. Where are the celebrated empathy skills of the designers when it comes to their own clients? Some have tried to awaken the business gene of design professionals – both as part of their training and as part of their encounter with the real world. In the provocatively titled book *Designers Are Wankers*, aimed at design students and practitioners, the author tries to cut it short:

> *Design is a business. You need to understand what business is and how it works. How do you plan to fit into that business? Essentially, if you are employed, you need to be worth more than you cost. If you are self-employed, you need to earn more than you spend. These basic facts apply to any business.*[9]

It's not that designers don't care. More likely, it has never occurred to them – and it certainly was not part of their training – that the well-being of their potential clients is the first prerequisite to be appreciated as a trusted supplier of a professional service.

Instead of investing some time in researching and developing narratives for what it would take to work with a company, designers tend to knock on their door and present a portfolio. Am I not talented…? Most designers are talented, and most designers would probably add valuable skills and input to most organizations they come into contact with, but for their counterparts – the manager or CEO of any given company – talent is not that easily spotted. They need reassurance that the designer understands the nature of their business, their challenges, and their goals.

One could hope that there is a shift happening, however slowly, toward a more harmonious relationship between the two parties. More and more designers find themselves working as members of multidisciplinary innovation teams, and as early as in design school they often contribute to projects taking place in partnerships between design schools, engineering schools, business schools, and industry partners. Through such collaborative projects, all partners start learning each other's languages, while at the same time challenging their individual prejudices.

---

[9]L. McCormack. 2005. *Designers Are Wankers* (London: About Face Publishing).

How Much Do Companies Know about Themselves?

Being aware that you need a designer who understands your company culture thus shouldn't discourage you from trying to find one. On the one hand, not all designers were trained in cocoons and with the ambition of stardom, and, on the other, you also want to make sure that you find a designer who can contribute with something that is not already present in your organization. Finding the right designer, however, also requires a deep understanding of where your own company comes from – how it was already designed and how its culture and identity were built. Where is it heading and what kind of designer can help you realize its dreams? What makes up its pillars and its intentions? Products or services or both; manufacturing or distribution; commodities or added value; marketing or sales; local, national, or global markets; incremental or radical changes…? Depending on who and what you are and on what you already have of skills, methods, and in-house expertise, what kind of designer you need and who would contribute the most to your success can vary greatly.

> *So just as there is a need for more understanding of business among designers, and a better understanding of what design is and what it can do among business people, there is also a need for a more profound understanding in many businesses of what they want to achieve and what can help them achieve it.*

Very often, this understanding comes gradually and either through accumulated experiences in one's organization or through confidence in documented experiences of others. However, it can be a long journey from not even considering design as a relevant component of one's business strategies to embracing design in a manner that unlocks the potential of design for one's company.

How Do Companies and Managers Articulate Their Needs for Design?

The first step is to realize that design is not a pastime – an art form and a matter of styling and facade. The next step is often to try – sometimes reluctantly – to engage a designer or a design firm to deliver a specific and narrowly defined output, such as packaging, a logo, an app, a website, a product, or even a store. From there on, one crucial factor is whether the experience is good and whether a direct correlation can be established between the designed element and its performance – whether a commercial benefit can be ascribed to it or not. If that connection is not firmly established, design tends to remain a matter of decorative enhancement rather than a strategically vital element. Another crucial factor is whether the designer or design firm exploits the situation to demonstrate the value of design beyond the aesthetics and functionality of the delivered solution. Is the brief answered uncritically, or does the design professional question where and how the most value is added? Are the given opportunities exploited – to prove how design is also a source of new thinking, a form of applied research, and an opportunity to challenge the existing, and not a creative skill and a maker's method alone?

There is a distinct difference between the awareness of design's role and importance in industries where design has always played a pronounced role – industries like fashion and luxury items, furniture, cars, and video game, and industries where design is a rather new notion. Such industries are often mechanical or engineering based, traditional service providers like banking and insurance, commodity-based industries, and many primary sectors, like agriculture and fisheries. The first category understands that there is no business without design and designers; it's part of their history and tradition, and it's a core element of their interface with the outside world. The second category might need much more time and conviction before they see the relevance of design for their own business and how design could become a part of their strategies.

At the same time, it needs to be said that some of the companies that have not only embraced design as a strategic asset, but that are also front-runners in using design, building a design culture, and benefiting from the competitive advantages that design can spur belong to the second category – companies such as Barclay's Bank and IBM, Carrefour, and Grundfos, the world's largest manufacturer of pumps.

Thesis # 3.

Q: Despite design thinking's popularity, is it still disconnected from the design industry…?

A: Perhaps we need to look at the interfaces between the two . . .

Then design thinking came about – or rather was discovered by the MBA community. This was no coincidence. Throughout the nineties, following a massive surge of digitization and globalization, new social structures, new buying patterns, and an emerging interest in behavioral economics and systemic thinking, design thinking suddenly came across as a viable approach to the challenges at hand. A new term, "Designomics," was introduced in 2010, which *Business Week's* Bruce Nussbaum explained as follows:

> *Designomics is important because both parts of the word – design and economics – are undergoing vast change as we speak. The global economy is emerging from the Great Recession, the worst recession since the Great Depression, with a very different shape, a very different trajectory and a very different set of growth engines. Design, with a capital 'D' is also emerging from the recent crisis, with a different form and function. A Design-based business model and a Design-based economy provide the best new opportunities for creating economic value, growth, revenues, profits, jobs and wealth for the decades ahead.*

And, in the same article,

> *Increasingly, people are turning to Design and creativity as a new paradigm to understand the needs and desires of changing cultures and creating entirely new options that never existed before. It is the ability to generate fresh concepts today that lead to new products, services and even social systems in healthcare, education and transportation tomorrow. In an era of cascading change that doesn't pause or end, Design is providing a pathway to the future.* [10]

Design thinking resonated, not only among business leaders, but also among public sector managers and policy makers. Our centralized systems – "factory world" – providing services for health, education, politics, and business support all have to be reinvented and decentralized

[10]B. Nussbaum. 2010. At the Design Indaba Conference, South Africa – from the Design Indaba News, May 1, 2010.

into more humane systems. The tools and methods embedded in design thinking – empathy, stakeholder engagement, cocreation and prototyping, constant rescoping, and reframing – all suddenly proved both pertinent and, surprisingly, to many, effective if managed properly. What this means, implicitly, is that there is an emerging new professional role, emulating that of the design manager, but coming out of and still belonging to the business domain – the manager designer. This happens when designers' skills become pertinent to reinvent the role of management, driven by the reinvention of organizational structures, the demand for speed and agility, and the changes that people management is undergoing. These changes call for less rigidity, more dialogue and engagement, experimentation, project-to-project process design, and reactivation of the senses in managing individuals, teams, and organizations. Design tools and design skills suddenly prove appropriate to fill in the gaps of classical management.

However, despite the tools and skills needed to manage exactly those kinds of processes – design management – already exist, they are still unknown to many. Thus, lots of talented people are currently engaged in reinventing the wheel – under new names and with new fancy models in their wake. The most obvious way of elaborating on what design thinking is and how it addresses the challenges of business and management is to portray two of the pioneers in making the concept accessible and relevant to those who could potentially benefit from it – businesses, organizations, and society at large. The first one, Tim Brown, has – among many other things – contributed by creating a language to help managers and others understand what design thinking is, while Alexander Osterwalder has contributed by showing people from all fields and sectors how design thinking can be applied and made tangible as an approach to assessing the potential of any business or any project.

Tim Brown

If anyone succeeded in entering into a meaningful conversation with industry leaders and thinkers from management, organizational theories, and innovation, there is no way around IDEO and some of the key individuals building the firm. The founding partners, the late Bill Moggridge,

David Kelley, and Mike Nuttall, all contributed to redefining the role and scope of design, putting the user at the center, while advocating the strategic importance of not only design as a skill but of design as a multidisciplinary methodology to create more meaningful, more profitable, and more lasting products and services. They all argued the value of "design thinking" as an approach after David Kelley reintroduced it as a business concept rather than belonging to its original domains – architecture and urban planning. The concept was already known from Peter Rowe's book *Design Thinking* from 1987 as well as from Bryan Lawson's *How Designers Think* from 1980 – both building on Herbert A. Simon's book from 1969 – *The Sciences of the Artificial*, introducing the idea, as earlier described, that design was actually "a way of thinking." A testimony to the position that IDEO had built through its first decade of existence was "The Hasso Plattner Institute of Design" at Stanford, commonly known as the d.school, developed as a collaborative project between IDEO, Stanford University, and Hasso Plattner, cofounder of the global software company SAP. From its inauguration in 2004 until today, thousands of C-suite business leaders from all over the world have acquired new insights and a new approach to running their businesses at d.school – based on the concepts of design thinking and framed to resonate with their already proven business practices. The d.school programs are based on eight principles, which could probably also be called the d.school "recipe" of design thinking – navigate ambiguity, learn from others (people and contexts), synthesize information, experiment rapidly, move between concrete and abstract, build and craft intentionally, communicate deliberately, and design your design work. Later on, we'll see that all the aforementioned are almost universally accepted as key elements of applying and benefiting from design thinking.

Tim Brown, IDEO's CEO from 2000 until quite recently, contributed to the proliferation of design as a proven approach to radical change, better bottom lines, and a better world in a way that can only be underestimated. Through articles and by contributing to the design discourse – both in the academic and in more popular domains, such as through TED Talks – and not least through his best-selling book *Change by Design: How Design Thinking Transforms Organizations and Inspires Innovation* – Tim Brown has achieved what few others did before him – becoming a business leader guru through a consistent message of what design can do. Citing directly from the resume, the book takes the following point of departure:

Design thinking is a collaborative process by which the designer's sensibilities and methods are employed to match people's needs not only with what is technically feasible and a viable business strategy. In short, design thinking converts need into demand. It's a human-centred approach to problem solving that helps people and organizations become more innovative and more creative.

This rather straightforward promise has resonated with business leaders as well as business magazines and journals. In their review of the book, *Business Week* said:

In his new book, the CEO of design shop IDEO shows how even hospitals can transform the way they work by tapping frontline staff to engineer change, - while the magazine Inc. seconded by stating that, This should be mandatory reading for marketers and engineers who can't understand why a product as cool as the Segway wasn't a breakout hit.

And the two testimonials somehow also capture the gist of Tim Brown's message to the world, as it is sharply cut in laying out the premises for the book:

The reason for the iterative, nonlinear nature of the journey is not that design thinkers are disorganized or undisciplined but that design thinking is fundamentally an exploratory process; done right, it will invariably make unexpected discoveries along the way, and it would be foolish not to find out where they lead. Often these discoveries can be integrated into the on-going process without disruption. At other times the discovery will motivate the team to revisit some of its most basic assumptions… seen not as a system reset but as a meaningful upgrade.[11]

[11]T. Brown. 2009. *Change by Design: How Design Thinking Transforms Organizations and Inspires Innovation* (New York, NY: Harper Collins), p. 17.

Through the book and his many other interfaces with a global audience of executives, Tim Brown managed to wipe away the skepticism surrounding the emerging fuzz around design thinking, resulting from all kinds of previous, however, not nearly as credible attempts, and which often added new misconceptions of what design thinking was, rather than a change of behavior and appreciation of design as a relevant approach to innovation and change.

Alexander Osterwalder

Another, and more recent, contributor to framing the role of design in a manner that has resonated broadly with both established businesses and in start-up communities – as well as in business support organizations throughout the world – is Alexander Osterwalder, a Swiss political scientist and business theorist and head of the consultancy firm Strategyzer. His contributions to a more holistic understanding of what it takes to succeed in business include the best-selling book *Business Model Generation* and his role as the lead creator of the omnipresent Business Canvas Model, on which his book is also based. This is a "paint-by-number" model that has proven valuable as a tool to ensure that new ventures – be they projects or start-ups – build on a minimum number of considerations, such as key partners, key activities and key resources, value propositions, customer relationships, customer segments and channels, and, finally, cost structure and revenue streams (Figure 5).

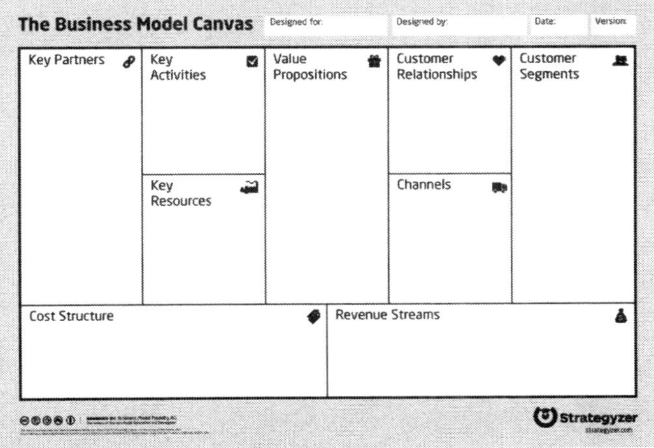

Figure 5 The Business Model Canvas

Source: A. Osterwalder and Y. Pigneur. 2010. The Business Model Canvas.

"A business model," according to Osterwalder, "describes the rationale of how an organization creates, delivers, and captures value."[12] Perhaps the main reason why this rather simple and highly accessible approach to business planning has resonated in business communities, design circles, and, not least, among educators of both design and business is the way it bridges the two domains. For one, it is a visual representation of what we otherwise know from thick reports and long reads and thus more easily embraced by designers (who in general are more apt at visual than verbal deciphering) and at the same time a refreshing reminder of textbook knowledge among people with business training. A second factor is the way that the development team attributes the tool – and its success – to a series of well-known designer skills, tools, and processes – cocreation, open design process, mood boards, paper mock-ups, visualization, illustration, and photography. And, as the "sales pitch" declares, the tool was cocreated by 470 strategy practitioners and was designed for doers – for those ready to abandon outmoded thinking and embrace new, innovative models of value creation: executives, consultants, entrepreneurs, and leaders of all organizations. That's music to the ears of anyone believing in design as an approach – not only to give form and shape to products, communication, and environments, but also to give direction and meaning to processes, organizations, and new ventures. The fact that Osterwalder comes from a business theory background – and has yet not only embraced design as a methodology and approach, but actually applied it directly onto the development of a business model mechanism – only proves that there is a certain rationale in exploring what design can do to other theories of management, innovation, organizational development, and learning.

This section describes a number of techniques and tools from the world of design that can help you design better and more innovative business models. A designer's business involves relentless inquiry into the best possible way to create the new, discover the unexplored, or achieve the

---

[12] A. Osterwalder and Y. Pigneur. 2009. *Preview version; Business Model Generation.* (Amsterdam, Self-Published)

functional. A designer's job is to extend the boundaries of thought, to generate new options, and, ultimately, to create value for users. This requires the ability to imagine 'that which does not exist'. We are convinced that the tools and attitude of the design profession are prerequisites for success in the business model generation.[13]

Thesis # 4.

Q: Is the myth that design cannot be measured discouraging you from managing design...?

A: Perhaps we need to better connect the benefits of design to business logics...

Design management includes all the elements of "classical" management disciplines and does not dodge the obligation of measuring and being measured on the benefits it brings or the value it creates. Several metrics for measuring the effect of design management have been developed and absorbed by the global design management community and others – to document and create a language for design management effectiveness. DME Awards[14] is a project that has existed since 2007 to assess and award excellent design management behavior. The assessment is based on a thorough questionnaire, on the basis of which each entry is judged as to its level of design management engagement; from no design management via design management as a project to design management as a function, and, ultimately, as a culture embedded throughout the organization. The model and thinking are inspired by and consistent with the original "design ladder,"[15] categorizing an organization's exploitation of design as being either "nondesign," "design as form-giving," "design as process," and "design as strategy." A comprehensive survey of design management practices in Europe was conducted by DME in 2009,[16] confirming the situational analysis made by the EU Commission the same year:

[13]A. Osterwalder and Y. Pigneur. 2009. *Preview version; Business Model Generation.* (Amsterdam, Self-Published)

[14]http://designmanagementeurope.com/

[15]Danish Design Centre. 2015. *The Design Ladder: Four Steps of Design Use* (Copenhagen: Danish Design Centre).

[16]https://www.bcd.es/site/unitFiles/2585/DME_Survey09-darrera%20versi%C3%B3.pdf

There is a clear potential to improve innovation performance and competitiveness at company and national level through the use of design.[17]

To determine the overall design management merits of an organization, five factors are scrutinized: awareness (of design and design management in the organization), planning (capabilities and engagement), resources (allocated to design and design management), expertise (both in-house and externally sourced), and, finally, process (to what extent it supports the strategies of the organization and its specific objectives). Over the ten years of case studies assessed and awards given, the overall observation is that when applied professionally and embraced by an organization's leadership, design management augments not only the benefits from applying design and design skills, but also the quality of the organizations' processes, project management, and performance.

The Designence Model[18]

In *The Handbook of Design Management*, the authors write that,

The Designence Model turns design into an activity of the organization and a resource that improves its organizational, knowledge and information capital.[19]

The model assumes four primary design objectives for business:

1. **Design as differentiator:** Design as a source of competitive advantage in the market through brand equity, customer loyalty, price premium, or customer orientation

---

[17]EU Commission. 2009. *Staff Working Document; Design as a Driver of User-Centred Innovation* (Brussels, Belgium: EU Commission).

[18]B. Borja de Mozota. 2005. *The Complex System of Creating Value by Design: Using the Balanced Scorecard Model to Develop a System View of Design Management from a Substantial and Financial Perspective* [The 6th European Academy of Design Conference "Design System Evolution"]. Bremen, Germany: University of the Arts; March 29-31.

[19]R. Cooper, S. Junginger and T. Lockwood, ed. 2011. *The Design Management Handbook* (London: Bloomsbury).

2. **Design as integrator:** Design as a resource that improves new product development processes (time to market, building coordination and consensus in teams, visualization skills); design as a process that favors a modular and platform architecture of product lines, user-oriented innovation models, and fuzzy-front-end project management
3. **Design as transformator:** Design as a resource for creating new business opportunities; for improving the company's ability to cope with change or (in the case of advanced design) as an expertise to better interpret the company's relationship with its larger environment and context and the marketplace. As a shared attribute, each of these three substantial design objectives can be measured financially with the help of design impact indicators.
4. **Design as good business**: Design as a source of increased sales and better margins, more brand value, greater market share, better return on investment (ROI); design as a resource for society at large (inclusive design, sustainable design). What we see emerging is design-driven leadership, as the skills and tools of designers inspire not only managers of processes and teams, but also senior level management – the CEOs, the COOs, and other C-suite members of larger organizations. The question is how the movement can be supported by evidence and best practice and also how it can be made more readily available to the members of senior management to see the value and potential of design thinking and design management.

There is a saying, often attributed to Peter Drucker, that "[i]f it cannot be measured, it cannot be managed." Some parts of the business community – namely large consultancy firms like Deloitte and others – maintain the argument as a key selling point of many of their services, whereas others question whether some of the subtler values of doing business, such as the resilience of corporate culture and the capacity to change and adapt, can be measured. Another popular version of the saying is "if you cannot measure it, you cannot improve it," which is seemingly relevant in a design context, as one definition of design often referred to is Hebert Simon's

Everyone designs who devises courses of action aimed at changing existing situations into preferred ones.[20]

Whether the metrics used are chosen for the purpose of management or change, the fact of the matter is that the existence of evidence to support its effectiveness is crucial for any concept, method, or investment to come across as credible in a business environment. Design has struggled with that. Despite an increasingly steady stream of reports from well-reputed government agencies and research institutes, the facts and figures – which have been consistently encouraging for decades now – have failed to resonate among business leaders to the extent that design has become a given. As an example, in 2015 Design Council in the UK, one of the most valuable sources of such research, assessed design's influence on the UK's gross value added, productivity, turnover, employment, and exports of goods and services, showing how design contributes significantly to the financial performance of businesses, regions, and local economies, as well as design workforce demographics.[21] And yet it just never seems to be enough...

As previously mentioned, there are mechanisms to measure the effectiveness of design on a company, and for most companies that measure would most probably come out as very positive if the design project was clearly defined, undertaken by the right design practitioners, and managed professionally. The challenge, in most cases, is getting them to a point where they are ready to invest in such an undertaking in the first place. Thus, we can conclude that measuring design effectiveness is valuable to reassure the board and to guide future projects – and alongside that, we can conclude that decades of convincing reports and large-scale evidence are not enough to incite the skeptics of design to change their perception of it. What can we do, then, instead of piling reports on top of reports? One approach would be to take the elevator down to the ground

---

[20]H.A. Simon. 1969. *The Sciences of the Artificial* (Cambridge, MA: MIT Press), 3rd edition 1996.

[21]Design Council. 2015. *The Design Economy: The Value of Design to the UK* (London: Design Council).

floor and ask ourselves, What do business leaders need, what is a business, and what makes up its logical framework and its cornerstones of evidence end truth? And how could design possibly fit into the corporate rationale and legacy?

Bridge

In this book, we aim to cast some light on the increasing blur that seems to have emerged alongside the aforementioned consolidation of design as a force and factor influencing the performance of organizations across sectors. Design thinking, although not entirely new, seems to have become during the last decade an MBA darling concept, which in many ways is the best news ever for design as a profession as well as an approach to finding meaningful answers to increasingly complex challenges. However, without anyone deliberately wanting to do so, design management seems to have lost momentum at the same pace at which momentum was gained by design thinking – almost as if they were mutually interchangeable and as if design thinking was, merely, design management version 2.0. Despite this, over the last decade, we have experienced a form of design renaissance that has changed not only how we talk about but, much more importantly, how we utilize design. The key to this shift is the extent to which design is now referred to as a strategic asset, enhancing user journeys and experiences by adding additional sensorial and aesthetic dimensions as well as adding meaning and trust to products, services, environments, and communication. "Design hence has the potential to act as a mediator between various links in any given value chain and as a response to the fear and uncertainty entailed by rapid change."

In the next part, we will systematically try to build bridges between, on the one hand, design thinking and design management and, on the on the other, universally embraced business approaches of Kim and Mauborgne (*Blue Ocean Strategy*), Hamel and Prahalad (*Competing for the Future*), Christensen (*Disruptive Strategy*), Chesbrough (*Open Innovation*), and Pine and Gilmore (*The Experience Economy*). Moreover, the fundamental ideas of Porter on competitive advantage, Argyris' works on organizational learning, Nonaka and Takeuchi's observations on the knowledge-creating company, Mintzberg's critical views on current organizational theories, and Weick's focus on sense-making will all be used as guiding lights and cornerstones on which our ideas about design excellence will be built. We will – as promised in the introduction and as a response to the described paradox – do what we can to

> ***build bridges between design thinking and design management on the one hand and universally embraced business approaches of a series of internationally acknowledged business gurus on the other.***

We believe that they represent the evidence that resonates with business leaders and managers around the globe. We also believe that their thinking and their models on management, innovation, and competitiveness, and on organizational development and learning all go perfectly well with what we believe that design, design thinking, and design management can do. We will not challenge any of their theories or models but will take the liberty of exploring what could happen if design were added to their thinking and what happens to their pool of evidence.

> *If we succeed in our mission, we will contribute to bridging design gurus and business gurus together, creating a common space and a common language of what design in a management context is and how design excellence can contribute to opening up new opportunities.*

PART 3

What seems clear is that to foster innovation, nurture your human capital, build digital and technological capabilities, improve your competitive advantage, and deliver memorable customer experiences, you need not only a robust and resilient culture, but also well-conceived and implementable strategies.

The Most Imminent Challenges of Management

We have now explored some of the possible barriers for uptake of design, design management, and design thinking in business. However, for design to resonate in boardrooms across the world, we also need to understand the challenges to which solutions – and the questions to which answers – are sought. On a day-to-day basis, the challenges facing managers and leaders of organizations will vary as greatly as the nature of their activities, the characteristics of their markets or audiences, and the strategies that they are pursuing. However, there are some universal challenges that are independent of sectors and strategic intents. In their 20th CEO Survey undertaken in 2017, the global consultancy firm PricewaterhouseCoopers (PwC) asked 1379 CEOs from 79 countries the following question: "Given the business environment you're in, which one of the following do you most want to strengthen in order to capitalize on new opportunities?" The most frequent answer was "innovation" – the most imminent concern for 23 percent of the CEOs asked. The next four areas of concern were "human capital," "digital and technological capabilities," "competitive advantage," and "customer experience."[1]

[1]PwC. 2017. *20th CEO Survey: 20 Years Inside the Mind of the CEO... What's Next?* (London, UK: PwC), p. 12.

These five main concerns correspond quite nicely with the areas of expertise and research represented by the aforementioned gurus:

- "innovation" (Kim & Mauborgne, Christensen, and Chesbrough)
- "human capital" (Argyris, Nonaka & Takeuchi, and Mintzberg)
- "digital and technological capabilities" (Weick)
- "competitive advantage" (Hamel & Pralahad and Porter)
- "customer experience" (Pine & Gilmore and Weick)

The fact that there are inherent inconsistencies between some of the ideas represented by the gurus will not keep us from recognizing all of the foregoing as equally important cornerstones of an aggregated legacy of what we'll refer to as "the gurus' thinking." As an example, one might argue that there is an inherent conflict between the fundamentals of blue ocean thinking, challenging and constituting an alternative to competitiveness, and the fundamentals of striving toward competitive advantage, as is the focus of other gurus. However, as the PwC survey shows, both innovation and competitive advantage are major concerns in the real world, leaving the cited gurus equally valid and important in our construct (Figure 6).

Figure 6 Linking Design Science to Key Business Strategies

Innovation

"Innovation" is a term used to describe the creation of something novel, which can be replicated and which in its applied form generates commercial or perceived value. According to Organization for Economic Cooperation and Development (OECD), there are four types of innovation[2]:

Product innovation: A good or service that is new or significantly improved. This includes significant improvements in technical specifications, components and materials, software in the product, user-friendliness, or other functional characteristics.

Process innovation: A new or significantly improved production or delivery method. This includes significant changes in techniques, equipment, and/or software.

Marketing innovation: A new marketing method involving significant changes in product design or packaging, product placement, product promotion, or pricing.

Organizational innovation: A new organizational method in business practices, workplace organization, or external relations.

The "**Blue Ocean**"[3] approach of Kim and Mauborgne prescribes that rather than competing within the confines of the industry or sector that you are already part of and trying to steal customers from rivals, you should focus on developing an uncontested market space that makes competition irrelevant. They claim that there are two ways to create such new spaces: either launch a completely new industry – which is rare and radical – or create a new space from within a red ocean by expanding the boundaries of an existing industry. Undoubtedly, radically changing the game by capturing either a market or niche that no one else has already occupied and expanding the boundaries of the market that one already competes within comes across as appealing to many companies. However, if blue oceans were easily found, they would quite rapidly turn red, one

[2]Oslo Manual. 2005. *Guidelines for Collecting and Interpreting Innovation Data* (Paris, France: OECD), 3rd ed.

[3]W.C. Kim and R. Mauborgne. 2005. *Blue Ocean Strategy: How to Create Uncontested Market Space and Make Competition Irrelevant* (Boston, MA: Harvard Business School Press).

ocean at a time. A challenge for most companies and their leaders, therefore, is to identify such opportunities – how to do it, how to manage, and whom to involve in such processes.

Another approach to innovation is "disruptive innovation,"[4] introduced by Clayton Christensen, as an alternative strategic path to the incremental improvements that characterize many categories. Continuous optimization of a product or service often tends to result in products that are too advanced for their audiences and often too expensive to be profitable, because the users are unable to appreciate, and hence also unwilling to pay for, all the advanced features offered. Disruptive innovation implies the introduction of a radically different solution to any given problem, rooted at the bottom of the market and then moving up and replacing the already existing propositions.

This approach to disruption is quite different than the more recent use of the word, which focuses on introducing something in the marketplace that thoroughly disrupts the market and leaves existing players obsolete. To clarify the difference between Christensen's original conception of the word "disruptive" and the more contemporary use of the word, in an interview with the web magazine *Inc.* in 2015,[5] he summarized his thoughts in five points:

- Disruptive innovation does not necessarily apply to every industry in which newcomers make the incumbents stumble.
- Disruption specifically refers to what happens when the incumbents are so focused on pleasing their most profitable customers that they neglect or misjudge the needs of their other segments.
- The disruption happens when the newcomer having already conquered the customers the incumbents are neglecting begins to conquer the high-margin customers too.
- Strictly speaking, Uber is not disrupting the taxi business.
- Disruption is a process, not a single moment or an isolated product introduction.

---

[4]C.M. Christensen. 1997. *The Innovator's Dilemma; When New Technologies Cause Great Firms to Fail* (Boston, MA: Harvard Business Review Press).

[5]Mochari, Inc. 2015. *The Startup Buzzword Almost Everyone Uses Incorrectly*, November 19, 2015.

However, the notion of disruptiveness – both in Christensen's interpretation of the concept and in the encyclopedic meaning of the word, on which the more current use is built – has proven its durability as a factor on the innovation agenda. That, however, does not make it easier for organizations to apply the concept in their own industries or product categories, and, as a result, a great majority of companies and organizations continue improving their propositions gradually and relentlessly in their daily struggle for market shares and profitability.

The third cornerstone related to innovation is the concept of "open innovation."[6] Berkeley professor Henry Chesbrough revived the concept, dating back to the sixties, in his book from 2003, and since then it has been an inevitable theme when discussing different approaches to innovation. The fundamental idea of open innovation is to engage both internal and external stakeholders in the pursuit of innovative products, services, and business models. The rationale acknowledges that valuable knowledge is available if entering into a dialogue with the market and with other players in the value chains that one belongs to, not least users and communities of users who possess insights that cannot be accessed through own research. Moreover, a more open approach to working with other companies in pursuit of some of the same goals as one's own organization can be valuable, for example through buying and selling licenses, establishing joint ventures or spin-offs, and entering into collaborative projects with universities and other players. The idea of open innovation has been embraced by both commercial organizations and public service providers, as it seems obvious that only very few organizations have the capacity to produce all the knowledge needed to undertake successful innovation. The barrier thus does not seem to be the acceptance of the concept but the knowledge of how to build the relations needed, how to engage them in the process, and how to capture and assess the input that can actually support the intentions of the undertaking.

The list of literature about innovation is massive. A Google Book search results in 714,000 hits, a number that is growing, clearly not indicating the number of individual titles published, but still indicating that

---

[6]H. Chesbrough. 2003. *Open Innovation; The New Imperative for Creating and Profiting from Technology* (Boston, MA: Harvard Business School Press).

the topic has enjoyed an overwhelming interest among researchers and commentators and, of course, that there is an insatiable market for such literature out there. Our choice of three titles and three approaches to the phenomenon thus reflects neither the diversity nor the depth of innovation as a topic. We do, however, qua their game-changing characters believe that the three angles will resonate broadly.

Human Capital

One of the most valuable assets for any company is its human capital – its people and their expertise. Finding the challenge of growing human capital to capitalize on new opportunities on the list is thus no surprise. Human resources management is more and more often associated with two other closely related concepts – organizational development and organizational design. Although also used to describe the correlation between the cost of education and the return through labor income, human capital is more often used in a much broader sense, and more true to the way that Adam Smith used it almost three hundred years ago: "the acquired and useful abilities of all the inhabitants or members of the society."[7] In a corporate context, human capital is the value represented by its staff members through their application of skills, know-how, and expertise – its combined human ability to solve business problems. As human capital in an organization exists only to the extent that its people choose to stay and devote their individual intellectual assets to benefiting the organization, attracting the right people with the right individual human capital and focusing on building their capacity and productivity is one part of the challenge. The other part is to create an organization that disposes of the optimal aggregated human capital to ensure not only the organization's collective productivity, but also its ability to innovate – as already discussed – and its competitive advantage, which we will discuss shortly. Many gurus have dedicated their research and professional practice to the capitalization of human capital.

Chris Argyris (1923 to 2013) dedicated a substantial part of his academic career to an area in which he was a pioneer – behavioral science

[7]T. Cadell. 1812. *The Works of Adam Smith: The Nature and Causes of the Wealth of Nations* (London, UK: Cadell & Davies).

and organizational development and how increased capitalization of the human capital can be achieved through organizational learning. Together with Donald Schön – the originator of *The Reflective Practitioner: How Professionals Think in Action*, thus the idea that the main objective of design is to explore and experiment – he developed the theory of "double-loop learning,"[8] which they described as "when organizational error is detected and corrected in ways that involve the modification of underlying norms, policies, and objectives." Argyris understood – long before many others – that creating an environment of learning, but also of constant organizational development, was a prerequisite for attracting, nurturing, and capitalizing on the most valuable human capital.

Human capital is often described as skills, know-how, and expertise – or as "the acquired and useful abilities" – as expressed by Adam Smith. Some of these useful abilities are not necessarily immediately available or communicable. The two Japanese researchers Ikujiro Nonaka, organizational theorist, and Hirotaka Takeuchi, Harvard strategy professor, found that there are two types of knowledge. On the one hand, there is the explicit knowledge that has been researched and documented, written down, and passed on. On the other, there is tacit knowledge, which is silent, acquired only by experience, and communicated only indirectly through metaphor and analogy. They explain the success of many Japanese companies by the fact that they have learnt how to transform tacit knowledge into explicit knowledge, thus increasing the aggregated human capital.

Our third guru with a focus on human capital is the Canadian academic Henry Mintzberg. However, he would probably disapprove strongly of that introduction, as a recent post on his own blog reads:

> *People are human resources. Not me! Feel free to let yourself be called a human resource. I am a human being, thank you. Not even a human asset, let alone human capital. Enough of the demeaning vocabulary of economics - turning us all into things. Resources are things we throw away when we no longer need them. Is that how to build a great enterprise: by throwing away the human beings?*[9]

---

[8] C. Argyris and D.A. Schön. 1974. *Theory in Practice* (San Francisco, CA: Jossey-Bass).

[9] H. Mintzberg. 2017. https://mintzberg.org/blog/half-truths-management, (March 22, 2017).

His research and writing have consistently and evolutionarily over more than 40 years revolved around the relations between management and managers, on the one hand, and organizational design and the role of the individual, on the other. And if one clear recommendation can be drawn from his massive production, it would be a single statement from one of his articles,

> *First, organizations are communities of human beings, not collections of human resources. As human beings, we engage with our communities. Indeed, we cherish the very sense of community, since it is the social glue that bonds us together for the social good, and so allows us to function energetically. Organizations thus work best when they too are communities, of committed people who work in cooperative relationships, under conditions of trust and respect.*[10]

To build such a community requires management strategies and managers who respect and care for the individual, commitment, and a true sense of responsibility. Mintzberg's ideas resonate among more and more individuals, as well as companies – perhaps in particular in organizations that have grown from start-ups into mature corporate cultures. But creating communities instead of more traditional organizations is demanding and not necessarily something that every manager or CEO is cut out to do.

Digital and Technological Capabilities

A digital strategy is a prerequisite for any meaningful strategy regardless of sector and industry. What challenges many, however, is the increasing complexity and speed of systems and solutions, and only a few managers without a strong background from an information and communications technology (ICT)-related professional environment will be able to see through the choices to be made – the upsides and downsides of alternative digital paths. Therefore, one of the key factors to exploiting the endless possibilities of digitalization is to attract the best possible staff, bringing

[10]H. Mintzberg. 2010. *Developing Naturally: From Management to Organization to Society to Selves* (Thousand Oaks, CA: Sage).

cutting edge and relevant knowledge into the organization – to help prepare the best possible strategies – and to constantly ensure that the organization does not lose momentum due to the absence of digital savviness. To enhance an organization's performance through digitalization is not just a matter of bits and bytes and of being a first mover. Crucial issues include determining the extent to which the products or services delivered in themselves can be partly or wholly digitalized; how to exploit digitalization to increase productivity and effectiveness of the delivery; and the role of digital as opposed to face-to-face engagement with clients, users, and other stakeholders and many others. The ICT influences financial, operational, and environmental performance; communication within the supply chain; market shares and access to new markets; effectiveness of working procedures; and the degree of organizational learning. We know this from numerous studies by amongst others De Groote and Marx, Su and Yang, and Kotelnikov, Meacham, Toms, Green Jr, and Bhadauria. At the end of the day, choosing the right technologies to invest in and how to prioritize the steps toward increased digitization build on a series of assessments, in terms of viability, feasibility, and customer experience. The latter is a separate issue but cannot be isolated from the digital and technological strategies of an organization.

Organizational theorist Karl E. Weick has dedicated his academic career to exploring concepts like loose coupling, sense-making, mindfulness, and organizational information theory. In particular, the second concept, sense-making, plays an important role when making decisions related to digitization and he introduction of new technologies, because both are key to successfully undertaking organizational change, and Weick's focus was exactly that – how we make sense of our surroundings, of complexity, and of the changes taking place around us.[11]

Complexity is a given and shouldn't be mixed up with complicating matters, as explained by researcher John Kamensky,

> *Understanding the difference between a complicated problem and a complex one is important for today's leaders. They require different*

[11]K.E. Weick. 1995. *Sensemaking in Organizations* (Thousand Oaks, CA: Sage Publications).

strategies and tools that are largely not interchangeable. Sometimes a problem will morph from one state to the other – either from complicated to complex, or vice versa – so you'll need to be ready to adapt your strategies and tools accordingly.[12]

Change is not a given, and it can be hard. That's probably why we recently came across a cartoon in an article on transformation, portraying a boardroom situation, where the chair says, "Instead of risking anything new, let's play it safe by continuing our slow decline into obsolescence." Fear of change is real, and Dutch researchers Henk Kleijn and Fred Rorink have identified the following seven most common and most significant psychological motives to resist change:

- "fear" (*I don't know if I can handle it*)
- "guilt" (*I could never subject my colleagues to this*)
- "alienation" (*will the change make me superfluous?*)
- "infringement" (*do I retain my privileges*?)
- "own needs" (*will the change hamper my career?*)
- "threat" (*this will weaken my position*)
- "uncertainty" (*I have no idea what this will mean to me*)[13]

Thus, in addition to all the more pragmatic challenges related to safeguarding the organizations' digital and technological capabilities, there are numerous factors that require an understanding of how people react to the changes and uncertainty that digitalization brings with it. Understanding the principles of sense-making and organizational information theory can facilitate such processes and minimize the potentially adverse effects of processes that are inevitable for most organizations to survive.

---

[12]J.M. Kamensky. 2011. *Managing the Complicated vs. the Complex*, IBM The Business of Government, Fall/Winter 2011, pp. 66-70.

[13]Kleijn and Rorink. 2005. *Verandermanagement : een plan van aanpak voor integrale organisatieverandering en innovatie* (*Change Management – a plan of approach for integrated organisational change and innovation*) (London, UK: Pearson Education).

Competitive Advantage

Despite some gurus' claim that striving for competitive advantages in any crowded category is futile, whereas only setting new standards and creating new spaces through disruptiveness and radical innovation secures the survival of a provider of products or services long term, the fact is that most organizations and most managers find themselves in a real-life situation, where competitors exist and where clients or customers have a choice, thus looking for the best proposition among many. An indisputable pioneer with regard to strategies for competitive advantage, and in many ways the guru over them all, is Michael Porter. Despite having influenced strategies across the world for almost four decades, he was appointed the most influential thinker by the "Thinkers50" – a recognized global ranking of management thinkers – both in 2005 and 2015, proving that his thinking is still as relevant as it was 40 years ago. One of his contributions is the "Five Forces"[14] analysis of an organization's competitiveness. This analysis focuses on "competitive rivalry" – mapping the number of competitors and the strengths of every single one of them, their products and services, and how they compare with yours. The second factor to be analyzed is "supplier power" – an analysis of how vulnerable you are to supply shortages, price increases, your suppliers' innovation, and quality. The third force is your customers' "buyer power" – their ability to drive your prices down and the strength they wield to dictate terms to you. The fourth factor to be analyzed is your organization's "threat of substitution." Is the solution that you offer likely to be replaced by another technology or a less costly process, which could threaten your position as a supplier? Finally, the analysis looks at the "threat of new entry" – both in terms of what the threshold is for entering the space that you're in and the likelihood of new suppliers entering your market with a more attractive proposition. By applying Porter's thinking and the Five Forces analysis, one gets not only a measure of the organization's competitiveness, but also a much clearer picture of which possible disruptions are on their way, which trends are dominating the market development, and

[14]M.E. Porter. May 1979. "How Competitive Forces Shape Strategy," *Harvard Business Review* 59, no. 2, pp. 137-45.

which business models seem to be the most sustainable within the sector or industry that you are operating in.

Another cornerstone for developing competitive strategies is the thinking of two other gurus, Gary Hamel and C.K. Prahalad – both well known from the previous list of top thinkers. Their approach to competitiveness is to look into the future to assess what your organization will look at in, for example, ten years from now. They pose some quite simple questions to inform that assessment, focusing on how the senior management look at the future, what issues they are concerned about, how your organization is viewed by your competitors, what your strengths are, whether you're trying to catch up or leading the pack, whether you have an agenda for transformation, and whether your time is spent maintaining your position or inventing the future. Based on how you respond to those questions – on a slide ruler – you get a clear impression of whether your company may be devoting too much energy to preserving the past and not enough to creating the future. Their thinking is based on the fundamental assumption that your competitiveness today does not reflect your competitiveness in the future:

> *The market a company dominates today is likely to change substantially over the next ten years. There's no such thing as "sustaining" leadership; it must be regenerated again and again.*[15]

So competitiveness – both here and now and not least when looking into the future – depends on strategies that are rooted in a thorough understanding of your own organization, its strengths and weaknesses, but also of the constant development in the marketplace of your supply chain and your competitors – the changes already taking place as well as those that can be envisaged in the next decade or so.

---

[15]G. Hamel and C.K. Prahalad. September 1994. *Competing for the Future*, Harvard Business Review, July-August 1994, adapted from the book *Competing for the Future* (Cambridge, MA: Harvard Business School Press).

Customer Experience

The fifth area identified by the CEOs in the PwC's survey as an area that needed to be strengthened in order to capitalize on new opportunities was customer experience. This rather abstract, and yet determining factor for whether your users choose the products or services you offer or whether they choose to go elsewhere, is not only important but also complex with transversal implications. Just before the turn of the millennium, Joseph Pine and James Gilmore were pioneers in articulating the changing role of experiences as something stretching way beyond the entertainment industries and transforming the playing field of business into what they called the experience economy. Their thinking was triggered by the increasingly prominent role of technology in raising the expectations of the customer, as well as by their own studies of consumer economic trends, showing that the behavior of consumers was increasingly motivated by the quality of the experience as an equally important parameter in the quality of the service or good itself. Their idea was that this development would have to trigger an evolution of products and services from commodity (characterized by undifferentiated products) to goods (characterized by distinctive, tangible things) to service (characterized by the activities you perform) to experience (characterized by the feeling customers get by engaging it), and, ultimately, to transformation (characterized by the benefit received by engaging).[16]

Customer experience – often abbreviated CX – and user experience – abbreviated UX – are often confused or used synonymously, as more and more interfaces between a supplier and a client – transactions, if we wish – are digital. However, UX is only one out of several elements of CX, focusing on usability, interaction design, and information architecture, enabling the completion of any desired task in a digital domain. Customer experience extends beyond that, encompassing interactions on all other platforms as well, including one-to-one customer service, advertising, pricing, delivery, and after-sales-service, as well as the perception of one's brand, what's being shared on social media, press coverage, and

[16]B.J. Pine and J.H. Gilmore. 1999. *The Experience Economy* (Boston, MA: Harvard Business School Press).

hearsay, even including experiences beyond firsthand encounters with the organization.

> *We identify four categories of customer experience touch points: brand-owned, partner-owned, customer-owned, and social/external/independent. The customer might interact with each of these touch point categories in each stage of the experience. Depending on the nature of the product/service or the customer's own journey, the strength or importance of each touch point category may differ in each stage.*

Especially, the social/external/independent touch points add complexity to the challenge:

> *These touch points recognize the important roles of others in the customer experience. Throughout the experience, customers are surrounded by external touch points, (e.g., other customers, peer influences, independent information sources, environments), that may influence the process. Peers may exert influence, solicited or unsolicited, in all three stages of the experience.*[17]

However, no matter how complex, a key to increasing one's competitiveness is the ability to craft coherent and integrated customer experiences. A crucial element in creating attractive customer experiences across platforms and touch point categories points back to another guru, Karl E. Weick, to whom we have already referred under *Digital and technological capabilities* and his work on sense-making. The concept has recently had a certain renaissance, and this time exactly in the context of creating meaningful customer experiences. The author, Christian Madsbjerg, who is partner in the consultancy firm RED Associates, in his newest book, makes the case for a more humanistic approach to understanding customers and markets, instead of relying entirely on algorithms and big data. He defines sense-making as "the ability to synthesize a lot of different kinds

---

[17]K.N. Lemon and P.C. Verhoef. November 2016. "Understanding Customer Experience Throughout the Customer Journey," *Journal of Marketing: AMA/MSI Special Issue* 80, pp. 69-96.

of data in order to make sense of a situation or a culture or a world"[18] or, one could add, a specific group of people – a segment or a market. And making sense is *the* purpose of design activity, according to some.[19] So working systematically with improving customer experience requires continuous optimization of all interfaces with the customer, based on the data available, but also the ability to synthesize and analyze that data in the context of understanding the motives and drivers of individuals or organizations.

Bridge

We have now tried to portray some of the design, design thinking, and design management paradoxes of our time and to pave the way for a discussion about how the fear of embracing it as a strategic framework for business development and change can be turned toward an urge to explore their potentials. We have also tried to paint a contemporary picture of the challenges that many companies face and the areas that CEOs from all over the globe mostly want to strengthen in order to capitalize on new opportunities. A popular phrase in management discussion forums for some time has been "culture eats strategy for breakfast," often attributed to Peter F. Drucker, without anyone having yet been able to trace the quote to him. What we know, however, is that Edgar H. Schein has said that "culture determines and limits strategy,"[20] which was probably meant to express the same idea. What seems clear, however, is that to foster innovation, nurture your human capital, build digital and technological capabilities, improve your competitive advantage, and deliver memorable customer experiences, you need not only a robust and resilient culture, but also well-conceived and implementable strategies.

---

[18]C. Madsbjerg. 2017. *Sensemaking: What Makes Human Intelligence Essential in the Age of the Algorithm* (Boston, MA: Little Brown Book Group).

[19]K. Krippendorff. 1989. "On the Essential Contexts of Artefacts or on the Proposition that 'Design is Making Sense (Of Things)," *Design Issues* 5, no. 2, pp. 9-39.

[20]E.H. Schein. 2004. *Organizational Culture and Leadership* (San Francisco, CA: Jossey-Bass Publishing).

PART 4

If successfully undertaken, the design process leads to an outcome where the aspirations of the designer go hand in hand with the needs and interests of the client and the overall concerns of society at large.

What Happens When Design Excellence Is Added to Strategy?

We have identified a handful of strategic challenges facing many – according to PwC, a majority – of the CEOs around the world, and in each one of the five areas, ***innovation, human capital, digital and technological capabilities, competitive advantage,*** and ***customer experience.***[1] An abundant range of literature exists to guide and comfort the leaders of this world's enterprises, and yet the case studies presented and the actions recommended are not always directly applicable to one's own situation as described. One might think that adding an additional layer to the tested and proven theories would make them even less likely to be adopted and applied by managers around the world. We beg to differ. Reframing is a common and extremely valuable component of the processes based on design thinking, and we believe that recontextualizing the literature referred to, researched, and written by some of the world's greatest gurus within the fields of strategic management, might add some new and valuable layers to their ideas, thus encouraging new

---

[1]PwC. 2017. *20th CEO Survey: 20 Years Inside the Mind of the CEO... What's Next?* (London, UK: PwC), p. 12.

audiences to try them out and already converted audiences to see them in a new light. To do so, we need to dig a little deeper into the two main components of our frame of thinking: design thinking and design management.

Design Thinking in Practice

Design thinking is an ***inspirer***. Although tons of books have been written about it over the last decade, and some have aspired to capture it in formulas and models, a group of researchers from the Hasso Plattner Institute in Potsdam found, through interviews with a number of design thinking experts, that "[w]hile the term 'Design Thinking' seems to allude to a common set of practices and a common theoretical matrix, the experts held ready an astonishing variety of understandings."[2]

Moreover, the experts had opposite beliefs with regard to several key issues within and interpretations of the concept. Fortunately, in the same research, a series of commonalities were also found, in particular an understanding that a strong focus on ***user needs***, a common understanding that the objective of design thinking is ***true innovation***, that ***reframing*** is an inevitable part of the process, and that ***multidisciplinarity*** and the presence of a ***positive communication culture*** are all pivotal elements of an undertaking under the "design thinking" label. Another question, which has been discussed vividly over the same period, is what design thinking actually is.

The most commonly used labels are method, approach, skill, or mindset – often used quite arbitrarily. An example can be found in an article in *Financial Times*, where the heading is "Design thinking – the **skill** every MBA student needs," and the subheading reads, "It is an important **mind-set** that lends itself to solving complex human problems." In the article, a third caption adds to the confusion: "They got here through design thinking – **creative strategies** used by designers that can be applied

[2]J. von Thienen, C. Noweski, C. Meinel, and I. Rauth (eds.). 2011. *The Co-evolution of Theory and Practice in Design Thinking – or – 'Mind the Oddness Trap!'* in *'Design Thinking: Understand – Improve – Apply'* (Heidelberg: Springer-Verlag).

to finding solutions for other issues."[3] In other contexts, design thinking has been referred to as a process:

> *Unlike the typical creative design* ***process****, which is usually an intuitive and individual process, design thinking consists of a flexible sequence of process steps and iteration loops, each including several tools and resulting in different artefacts.*[4]

Richard Buchanan even introduces the concept of technology as a relevant label:

> *Indeed, the variety of research reported in conference papers, journal articles, and books suggests that design continues to expand in its meanings and connections, revealing unexpected dimensions in practice as well as understanding. This follows the trend of design thinking in the twentieth century, for we have seen design grow from a trade activity to a segmented profession to a field for technical research and to what now should be recognized as a* ***new liberal art of technological culture****.*[5]

Depending on how it is applied, within which context and with which motives, design thinking can be any of the aforementioned. In his book from 2009, Roger Martin somehow applies a more grounded approach to design thinking, labelling it as what is claims to be – a way of ***thinking***; one that merges analytical thinking with "the randomness" of intuitive thinking, thus exploiting both existing knowledge and the exploration of the unknown.[6] This notion aligns quite well with the views of the late Bill

---

[3]I. Stigliani. 2017. "Design Thinking – The Skill Every MBA Student Needs," *Financial Times*, June 22, 2017.

[4]K. Thoring and R. Müller. 2011. *Understanding Design Thinking: A Process Model Based on Method Engineering* [International Conference on Engineering and Product Design Education]. London, UK; September 8-9, 2011.

[5]R. Buchanan. October 1990. *Wicked problems in design thinking.* Paper presented at 'Colloque Recherches sur le Design: Incitations, Implications, Interactions', Vol. VIII, no. 2, Spring 1992.

[6]R.L. Martin. 2009. *The Design of Business: Why Design Thinking is the Next Competitive Advantage* (Boston, MA: Harvard Business Press).

Moggridge, one of the founders of IDEO. In an interview with one of the authors of this book back in 2008, he stated:

> *The core skills of the designer are the abilities to lay out alternatives, to visualize them, to choose between alternatives and to give their solution some kind of tangible representation. While anyone can tap into design thinking with his own skills and background knowledge, designers do it as part of their professional approach. Others need to adapt to it, but all of us represent - just like an iceberg - a tip of logics, articulate skills and methodologies, but underneath that, an incredible resource of tacit knowledge and intuition. Having the courage to access this reservoir and to try out the ideas that emerge from it is design thinking. As I see it, design thinking is merely* ***a licence to apply intuition to your processes****.*[7]

However, whether it is a process in its own right or not, design thinking fits well with processes of development and change, and to benefit from design thinking, access to a series of skills is needed – the skills to engage stakeholders and moderate ideation processes; to visualize and prototype based on verbal input; to plan and structure; and to manage a flow of information, consecutive loops and iterations, different forms of expertise and technological, economic, and human resources. All of those are skills, which require certain types of training and experience to master, and very few master them all. Skills and tools are intrinsically linked, and some skills are tools, such as visualization;

> *...visualisation is really a "meta tool" so fundamental to the way designers work that it shows up in virtually every stage in the processing of designing for growth....It is an approach for identifying, organizing and communicating in ways that access "right brain" thinking while decreasing our dependency on "left brain" media such as numbers . Visualisation consciously inserts visual imagery into our work processes and focuses on bringing an idea to life, simplifying team*

---

[7]B. Moggridge. 2008. *It's all about Design Thinking* – Inform 3-2008 (Copenhagen: Danish Designers).

collaboration and eventually creating stories that go to the heart of how designers cultivate empathy in every phase of their work and use it to generate excitement for new ideas.[8]

Visualization is only one of the tools, native to the design process, that has been broadly adopted – as have some of the visual representations of what a development process looks like; from IDEO's popular three circles diagram or the Double Diamond, developed by the British Design Council. Organizations often intelligently change these phases into four questions and combine the questions with the most pertinent design methods for each question:

- ***What is? Mapping journeys and value chain analysis, mind mapping, and brainstorming***
- ***What if? Concept development, scenarios, and narratives***
- ***What works? Prototyping, stakeholder engagement, and cocreation***
- ***What wows? Assumption testing, rapid prototyping, learning launch***

At least one of those should be visualization based, insisting on the importance of materiality, which is not often part of business routines. Every idea has a form, which goes back to our introduction on how design science differs from business science. Business science and economics are based on numbers, while design science is based on pragmatic semiotics, talent for drawing and visuality.

Nonetheless, they are all key skills to undertake successful design management. Moreover, to benefit from design thinking, a methodological framework is needed. This might be standardized or bespoke, as long as all key players in the process understand and embrace the chosen protocol. It seems difficult to claim that design thinking in itself is such a framework, because it – as already discussed – takes on a broad variety of forms and interpretations.

---

[8]J. Liedtka and T. Ogilvie. 2011. *Designing for Growth* (New York, NY: Columbia Business School Publishing).

Although design thinking might not in itself be a mindset, there is no doubt that it does require a growth mindset to foster change and innovation. According to the bestselling author, Dr. Carol S. Dweck, there are only two fundamental mindsets; a *fixed* mindset and a *growth* mindset. Having a growth mindset means, according to the author, that "the hand you're dealt is just the starting point for development."[9] This mindset is needed to believe in the explorative nature of a design process – seeking opportunities and gold, where nobody else found it before you.

> *Designers are exploring concrete integrations of knowledge that will combine theory with practice for new productive purposes, and this is the reason why we turn to design thinking for insight into the new liberal arts of technological culture.*[10]

Design thinking ***inspires***. However, by reflecting the visions and aspirations of an organization, it also entails a mandate to work with design and designers, thus ***empowering*** the organization and its management to explore the potential of exploiting design methodologies, design processes, and design management, and, in turn, the powerful embodiment of good design.

Design Management in Practice

Design management is an ***enabler***. It serves as a mechanism to engage stakeholders; to manage data, time, and resources; to ensure continuous learning as the project progresses; and to guarantee coherence with the strategic aims and objectives of the design project. It can be applied on an operational, functional, and strategic level, but its overall aim is to enable and deliver at each defined stage of the design process, which could look like this:

---

[9]C. Dweck. 2006. *Mindset: Changing the Way You Think to Fulfil Your Potential* (New York, NY: Random House).

[10]R. Buchanan. October 1990. *Wicked problems in design thinking*. Paper presented at 'Colloque Recherches sur le Design: Incitations, Implications, Interactions', Vol. VIII, no. 2, Spring 1992.

- ***Identify the problem***
- ***Identify criteria and barriers***
- ***Generate ideas for possible solutions***
- ***Explore realistic scenarios***
- ***Choose among alternatives***
- ***Prototype***
- ***Test and refine***
- ***Produce, execute, or launch***

What, then, specifically, is the role, and what are the challenges of design management? One way of summarizing it could be to merge the operational, functional, and strategic levels, based on "The Design Manager's Toolbox," as presented in *Design Management – Using Design to Build Brand Value and Corporate Innovation* by Brigitte Borja de Mozota:

Strategy: Align design strategies with overall organizational strategies, objectives, and goals; define the role of design in products, services, user experience, communication, and brands; and coordinate design strategies with the marketing, innovation, or R&D and communications departments.

Planning: Allocate sufficient resources to draft detailed design briefs for each design project; choose the most relevant methodologies and processes; define procedures, design and quality standards, schedules, and resources, as well as measurable success indicators, observing the objectives and strategies of the organization, its complexity, and resources.

Structure: Embed ownership of the design process at the top management level, and define the roles and tasks of internal as well as external designers and design managers.

Finances: Estimate key figures and financial procedures as well as realistic budget for each design process to be used for planning, continuous monitoring, and final audit and evaluation purposes, to ensure correspondence with the intentions of the design strategy and the individual design brief.

Human Resources: Define which specific design competences your organization needs, strive to create a mindset, which is favorable to design and design thinking throughout the organization, and keep your design strategies in mind when hiring new staff, while constantly assessing the potential for and benefits of engaging existing staff from across the organization in design processes.

Information: Make sure that your design strategies are known to all members of your organization, and allocate resources to monitor new design trends and technologies.

Communication: Consider design competitions as a source of concepts and ideas; communicate new design projects and solutions internally and to external stakeholders; and establish procedures to encourage cross-disciplinary working relations both internally and with suppliers, knowledge partners, and others.

For many, all this looks familiar, as all the foregoing would resonate with any professional who has worked as a project manager. What differ from many other similar roles are the biases of what design is and what it can do. Not all of us understand the details of the CRM or QA systems of our organization, but few of us would even think about questioning the importance of customer relations or quality assurance. Design, however, is often questioned, and that adds a layer of advocacy to the professional role of anyone representing design in domains where it is not already fully embraced. And even though the overall idea of design resonates with an organization's management, uncertainties seem to exist as to how to get started or how to ensure a real benefit from working with designers.

> *Design has the potential to play an even greater role in economic growth in future: Three-fifths of respondents (59%) believe that design will contribute substantially to any of a range of business improvement activities in the next three years. This includes efforts to increase sales in the UK, the development of new products or services, and marketing campaigns. Yet design offers much more than this, and despite awareness of its potential benefits a sizeable proportion of businesses still do not use design as effectively as they could.*[11]

---

[11]Design Council. 2018. *The Design Economy 2018, The State of Design in the UK* (London, UK: Design Council).

Actually, the number of companies that work strategically with design comes nowhere close to that. The figures from the aforementioned UK study show that although 40 percent of the respondents do not apply design at all, only 10 percent use it strategically. A similar study from Denmark confirms the picture, showing that whereas a little over half of all companies in Denmark use design, only 13 percent use it strategically and as a driver of their business development.[12] This, of course, makes one wonder where the reasons for this gap should be found. There are several reasons. In the aforementioned Danish study, 86 percent of the companies that do not use design at all say that the most important reason is that they do not see design as relevant for them and their business – followed by uncertainty of which value design adds, and lack of evidence for return on investment. Hence, the top three all refer to the expectancy of actually benefiting from the use of professional design services, whether internal or external. Another, perhaps more interesting, question is why the companies that have actually embarked on the use of design are not exploiting its potential to its fullest – despite acknowledging what design, applied strategically, can actually do to "stay competitive in the current economic climate." These could be some, however possibly not as easily admitted,

- *not knowing enough about what design is, thus feeling unapt at procuring it as a professional service*
- *not being entirely clear on what the need is, thus being afraid of paying for a lot of fuzziness at best and nothing at worst*
- *not having clear ideas of where to start, what to expect from the process, or desired outcomes*
- *not being able to assess good design from bad or the quality of the delivery, thus being afraid of revealing incompetence*

Most of us would recognize one or more of those reservations from one area or another; we are not very good at commissioning skills or services of which we know very little, and when, in addition to that, it is not always entirely clear up front what the problem or challenge is, justifying an investment in design can be difficult for some.

[12]Danish Design Centre. 2016. *Exploring Design Impact* (Copenhagen: Danish Design Centre).

Half a century ago, the renowned designer couple Ray and Charles Eames articulated a model for what they considered "good design."[13] The diagram was developed for the 1969 exhibition "What is Design?" at the Musée des Arts Décoratifs in Paris, France, with the objective of explaining how "good design" is achieved, designs that simultaneously balance the needs and interests of the client, the design office, and society as a whole (Figure 7).

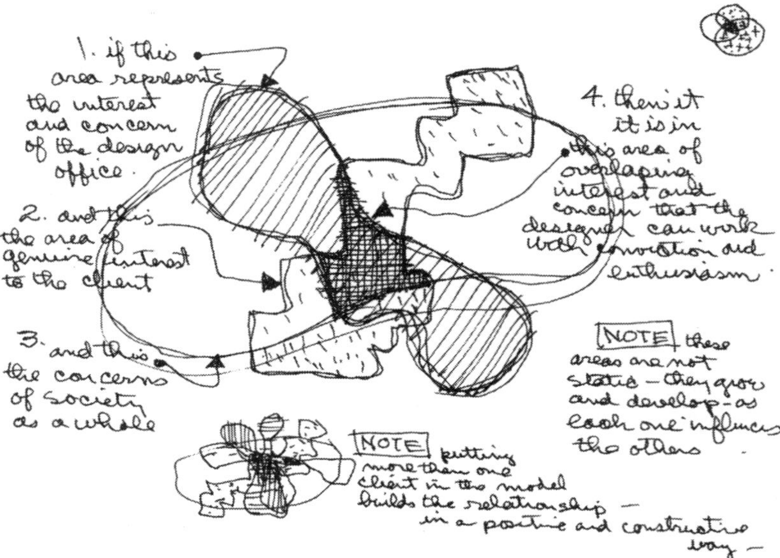

Figure 7 The Eames Design Process Diagram

Design Thinking and **Design Management** are largely the mechanisms needed to achieve this; to manage all the factors influencing whether the solution achieves the goals it set out to resolve. If successfully undertaken, the design process leads to an outcome where the aspirations of the designer (of creating meaningful products and services, making the world more beautiful and people's life easier, humanizing technology, and improving user experience) go hand in hand with the needs and interests of the client (differentiation, competitiveness, brand positioning,

[13]Eames. 1969. *Design Process for the "What is Design"*, Louvre, Paris

effectiveness, and profitability) and the overall concerns of society at large (protecting the planet and eradicating poverty, famine, and disease).

The Designence model™,[14] as previously introduced, proves an appropriate measure, because good design serves as a **differentiator**; a source of competitive advantage in the market through brand equity, customer loyalty, price premium, or customer orientation; as an **integrator,** improving new product development processes and favoring a modular and platform architecture of product lines, user-oriented innovation models, and fuzzy-front-end project management; as a **transformation factor** allowing the creation of new business opportunities and improving the company's ability to cope with change; and, finally, as a vehicle for **good business** – fostering increased sales and better margins, more brand value, greater market share, and better return on investment.

The father of the Stage-Gate development model, Robert G. Cooper, has summarized the critical factors determining success or failure of a new product or service as (1) Doing the *right projects* and (2) Doing *projects right.*[15] Many would claim that, by and large, we are far better at doing projects right than at doing the right projects, but real change is achieved only when the two go hand in hand. **Design Thinking** – inspiring meaningfulness, relevance, and attractiveness – ensures that we do the right projects and empower the organization to pursue design as a strategic measure, whereas **Design Management** brings innovation and creativity to life and makes sure that we do projects right. Both are key components of what could also be referred to as **Design Excellence.** However, one vital element needs to be added to complete the equation: **Design**. Design, while encompassing elements of strategic considerations, is essentially the ***embodiment*** of the visions, strategies, and ideas of an organization.

Thus, we go all the way back to what Herbert Simon, Donald Schön, Willemien Visser, and Don Norman have in common, the understanding of design as a tangible representation of ideas: Simon – "The intellectual

---

[14] B. Borja de Mozota. 2005. *The complex system of creating value by Design: Using the Balanced Scorecard model to develop a system view of design management from a substantial and financial perspective,* The 6th European Academy of Design Conference "Design System Evolution", University of the Arts, Bremen, Germany, March 29-31.

[15] G. Cooper. April 1999. "From Experience: The Invisible Success Factors in Product Innovation," *Journal of Product Innovation Management* 16, no. 2, pp. 115-33.

activity that produces **material artefacts** is no different fundamentally from the one that prescribes remedies for a sick patient or the one that devises a new sales plan for a company or a social welfare policy for a state"[16]; Schön – "When someone reflects in action, he becomes a **researcher in the practice context**"[17]; Visser – "...designing is most appropriately characterised as a **construction of representations**"[18]; and Don Norman – "The move from craft-based to evidence-based design, from simple objects to complex sociotechnical systems, and from craftspeople to design thinkers suggest that we are now faced with a fork in the road with two different possible futures for design: (1) **A craft and practice**; (2) A mode of thinking."[19] They all focus on design requiring some form of output, an embodiment. Thinking is not enough; the thinking must be challenged and tested and embodied one way or another to be labelled design. Hence, ***design excellence*** requires a clear mandate to embrace design; ***empowerment,*** the knowledge and structures needed to work strategically with design; ***enablement,*** the skills, creative capacity, and tools to explore and materialize the visions of the organization; ***embodiment*** in the form of tangible representations of design.

What Happens When Design Excellence Is Added to Strategies for the Five Areas?

In this section, we will discuss the role and effect of design excellence – of design as inspiration as well as enabler – in the context of ***innovation***, ***human capital, digital and technological capabilities, competitive advantage,*** and ***customer experience*** – as a response to the challenges of management, as discussed in a previous chapter. Our aspiration is to

[16]H.A. Simon. 1988. "The Science of Design: Creating the Artificial," *Designing the Immaterial Society* 4, no. 1/2, pp. 67-82.

[17]D. Schön. 1983. *The Reflective Practitioner: How Professionals Think in Action* (New York, NY: Basic Books).

[18]W. Visser. 2007. "Designing as Construction of Representations: A Dynamic Viewpoint in Cognitive Design Research," *Human-Computer Interaction* 21, no. 1, pp. 103-52.

[19]D.A. Norman. 2016. *The Future of Design: When You Come to a Fork in the Road, Take It* (jnd.org).

argue the relevance, role, and value of ***design excellence*** as a key vehicle for successful growth through strengthening the organizations' capabilities within each of the five contexts.

Innovation Strategies: How Design Excellence Contributes to Foster Innovation

There are many claimed drivers of innovation, or rather reasons for engaging in innovation activities. Some of these reasons could be financial pressures to decrease costs, increase efficiency, do more with less; increased competition; shorter product life cycles; value migration; stricter regulations; industry and community needs for sustainable development; increased demand for accountability; community and social expectations and pressures (giving back to the community, doing good, etc.); demographic, social, and market changes; rising customer expectations regarding service and quality; greater availability of potentially useful new technologies coupled with the need to keep up or exceed the competition in applying these new technologies; and the changing economy.[20] Moreover, as previously mentioned, Organisation for Economic Cooperation and Development (OECD), in its Oslo Manual, defines four different kinds of innovation – product, process, marketing, and organizational innovation – while defining innovation as

> *The implementation of a new or significantly improved product (good or service), or process, a new marketing method, or a new organizational method in business practices, workplace organization or external relations.*[21]

That's not it. There are also different types or degrees of innovation: *basic research, sustaining innovation, breakthrough innovation, and disruptive innovation,* all characterized by different objectives and activities.[22]

---

[20]G. Hamel. 2000. *Leading the Revolution* (Boston, MA: Harvard Business School Press).

[21]OECD. 2005. *Oslo Manual: Guidelines for Collecting and Interpreting Innovation Data* (Paris, France: OECD).

[22]G. Satell. 2017. *Mapping Innovation: A Playbook for Navigating a Disruptive Age* (New York, NY: McGraw Hill).

Finally, there has been an evolution over the last five decades with regard to the overall rationale of investing in innovation, as measured by the sources of competitive advantage:

- In the 1960s and 1970s, the focus was on *Making things cheaper,* exploiting the advantage of cost reductions, mass production, and division of labor.
- In the 1980s and 1990s, the focus shifted to *Making things better,* taking advantage of new technologies, manufacturing models, and automation to increase product quality and speed.
- Since the turn of the century, the focus has been on *Making better things,* harvesting the benefits of better design, smarter solutions, uniqueness, and authenticity.[23]

Although technological advances, making the development of new products and services more efficient and the marvel of what could be done, were the main drivers of innovation for decades, innovative activities today most often start with the needs and aspirations of the user. Several terms, reflecting slightly diverse approaches, are used, such as user-driven, user-centered, and user-oriented. What they have in common is that they see the user – in its broadest sense – as a resource that informs the development of new products, services, or processes of innovation. The way in which these stakeholders are engaged, however, differs, from studies and observations via combinations of direct and indirect influence on the development process to actual cocreation. In any case, design plays a vital role in making such processes work and in ensuring that the information gathered during the course of the process is framed and reframed to truly reflect real needs and opportunities that justify the investment in an innovative process. Design's role as a lever of innovation is articulated quite precisely in an article by Robert W. Veryzer and Brigitte Borja de Mozota:

As products continue to embody progressively complex technologies and to offer a myriad of capabilities, it is often the user's ability to

[23]Rosenfeld, Regional Technology Strategies, Inc. 2006.

understand and to appreciate the product that stands as a principal design constraint as well as being a key element in marketplace success.[24]

The role of design, as well as some kind of engagement of users, in the pursuit of fostering innovation is widely recognized, and yet there are still divergent ideas as to which "methodology" is the most valuable. The answer is probably to be found as a result of an assessment of each individual project or challenge. That assessment in itself calls for design management: to moderate and manage the process of choosing the optimal "protocol," for any given project – whether its outcome objective is tangible or intangible. When the project has been clearly defined, the role of design excellence is to cater to the needs and conditions of the project team, to inspire and inform, and to manage the process as meticulously as any other investment in the organization would be managed. Even though already argued, it is crucial to understand that there is a direct correlation between the ***management*** of the process and the quality and value of the outcome. This was one of the conclusions after a study of different levels of user involvement, measured by the amount and quality of ideas generated:

The study has concluded that user involvement in service innovation, if properly managed, has a positive effect on the quality of the created service ideas and obtains valuable use information. Companies that learn how to use the potential of user involvement will gain a competitive advantage.[25]

Latching this up onto Kim & Mauborgne's ***Blue Ocean***[26] approach, after the book became a global success, not only their readers, but also

---

[24]R.W. Veryzer and B. Borja de Mozota. 2005. "The Impact of User-Oriented Design on New Product Development: An Examination of Fundamental Relationships," *Journal of Product Innovation Management* 22, pp. 128-43.

[25]P.R. Magnusson, J. Matthing, and P. Kristensson. November 2003. "Managing User Involvement in Service Innovation Experiments With Innovating End Users," *Journal of Service Research*, 6, no. 2, pp. 111-24.

[26]W.C. Kim and R. Mauborgne. 2005. *Blue Ocean Strategy: How to Create Uncontested Market Space and Make Competition Irrelevant* (Boston, MA: Harvard Business School Press).

the authors realized that there was still a long way to go to understand what it takes to do it, how to manage, and whom to involve in such processes. The result of this realization was a sequel, focusing more on what it actually takes to move beyond competition.[27] In an interview with *Forbes*, they stress the role of creative competences to actually pursue a Blue Ocean strategy:

> *Existing strategy work has been virtually silent on the role of people and our human spirit in creating growth. Yet, our research shows that making a blue ocean shift is a transformational journey that requires a balance of hearts and minds, of humanness, confidence, and creative competence. For any process to work, it must acknowledge our doubts and build our confidence as much as unlock people's requisite creativity.*[28]

Unlocking people's creativity is a pivotal objective of user-oriented design processes and one of the hallmarks of designers, and the facilitation and management of such processes rest at the heart of design management.

On the same note, latching what we know about the effects of design excellence onto Clayton Christensen´s thinking around ***disruptive innovation,***[29] even a "traditional" business consultancy like Accenture advocates the role of not only design, but also designers, as being instrumental in the process of disruptive innovation;

> *Designers use their awareness of customer wants and needs to conceptualize high-value and differentiated offerings. They draw on existing off-the-shelf components as well as leading-edge innovations to create novel blueprints that satisfy customers.*[30]

---

[27]W.C. Kim and R. Mauborgne. 2017. *Blue Ocean Shift Beyond Competing: Proven Steps to Inspire Confidence and Seize New Growth* (New York: Hachette Books).

[28]Forbes Magazine. 26 September 2017. *W. Chan Kim And Renée Mauborgne: How to Shift from A Red to a Blue Ocean.*

[29]C. Christensen. 1997. *The Innovator's Dilemma: When New Technologies Cause Great Firms to Fail* (Boston, MA: Harvard Business Review Press).

[30]P.F. Nunes and J. Bellin. 2015. *Thriving on Disruption* (Dublin: Accenture Outlook).

Finally, the concept of Chesbrough's ***open innovation***[31] goes extremely well with design excellence, requiring active engagement of both internal and external stakeholders in the pursuit of innovative products, services, and business models. Bringing multiple stakeholders together, however, is not always easy and requires the right skills and tools – not least with regard to framing the project as well as the interests of various stakeholders:

> *When initiating open innovation, framing both the collaboration and the design space is required. Framing a design space is making explicit possible embodiments of a value proposition while framing a collaboration space is clarifying the motivations and defining boundaries between a group of profit and/or non-profit organizations.*[32]

Design excellence – framing and reframing being central elements – not only enhances, but also inspires and enables organizations to benefit from open innovation processes. Hence, regardless of which approach to innovation an organization prefers: whether incremental, radical, or disruptive and whether open or closed, the role of design, well inspired and well managed, is documented, thoroughly tested in real-life environments, and only rarely disputed.

Human Resources Strategies: How Design Excellence Helps Harvesting from Investments in Human Capital

Although the innovation and design of products and services are embraced by many organizations, the concept of organizational design has been far less attended to. Originally, organizational design focused on designing appropriate structures, but this has slowly evolved into several more complex and integral operations.

---

[31]H. Chesbrough. 2003. *Open Innovation; The New Imperative for Creating and Profiting from Technology* (Boston, MA: Harvard Business School Press).

[32]O.T. Plasencia, Y. Lu, S.E. Baha, P. Lehto, and T. Hivikoski. 2011. *Designers initiating open innovation with multistakeholder through co-reflection sessions.* Proceedings from 'Diversity and Unity' – IASDR2011 – the 4th World Conference on Design Research, Delft.

Organisation design is not simply about mapping out an organisational structure, but also about how the organisation is aligned with all other aspects, functions, processes and strategies within the business.[33]

A more current focus is rather on designing well-functioning teams, processes, and relations. That probably sounds like a challenge vested safely in the "human resource" department, but that as well is a somewhat outdated view on organizational dynamics. The global consultancy Deloitte, in its 2016 edition of the *Global Human Capital Trends* report, based on more than 7,000 responses to their survey in over 130 countries around the world, captures one of the most dominant trends in human resources management:

Executives are embracing digital technologies to reinvent the workplace, focusing on diversity and inclusion as a business strategy, and realizing that, without a strong learning culture, they will not succeed. Amidst these changes, the Human Resources function is taking on a new role as the steward and designer of these new people processes.

and

Human Resources is being asked to simplify its processes, help employees manage the flood of information at work, and build a culture of collaboration, empowerment, and innovation. This means that Human Resources is redesigning almost everything it does - from recruiting to performance management to onboarding to rewards systems. To do this, our research suggests that Human Resources must upgrade its skills to include the areas of design thinking, people analytics, and behavioral economics.

Moreover, the survey shows that

---

[33]J. Stewart and P. Rogers. 2012. *Developing People and Organisations* (London, UK: Kogan Page).

> *Respondents at companies where HR delivers the highest levels of value are almost five times more likely to be using design thinking in their programs than their peers.*[34]

The survey also shows that design thinking is used to strengthen ***organizational design*** when restructuring roles or the organization itself; ***engagement*** to make work easier, more efficient, more fulfilling and more rewarding; ***learning*** to put the user experience ahead of the process; ***analytics*** to recommend better solutions directly to the individual employee; ***HR skills*** to upgrade understanding of digital design, mobile application design, behavioral economics, machine learning, and user experience design; and ***digital HR*** to develop new digital tools that can make work easier and better. This resonates perfectly well with Argyris' *double-loop learning,*[35] focusing on "the modification of underlying norms, policies, and objectives" and on creating an environment of learning and constant organizational development, as well as with Nonaka's and Takeuchi's *knowledge-creating company,*[36] acknowledging the value of nurturing and further developing explicit knowledge that has been researched and documented, written down and passed on, as well as tacit experience-based knowledge. It also reflects the respect and care for the individual, commitment and true sense of responsibility, argued by Mintzberg to support the idea of organizations performing at their best "when they too are communities, of committed people who work in cooperative relationships, under conditions of trust and respect."[37]

In a report from 2011, The Institute for the Future forecasts the drivers of the future as well as the corresponding ten most important skills needed to deliver on those drivers. Out of those, at least a handful are key skills that are normally dedicated to professional design

---

[34]Deloitte Development LCC. 2016. *Global Human Capital Trends 2016: The New Organization: Different by Design* (New York, NY: Deloitte Development LCC).

[35]M. Argyris and D. Schön. 1974. *Theory in Practice* (San Francisco, CA: Jossey-Bass).

[36]I. Nonaka and H. Takeuchi. 1995. *The Knowledge-Creating Company: How Japanese Companies Create the Dynamics of Innovation* (Oxford: Oxford University Press).

[37]H. Mintzberg. 2010. *Developing Naturally: From Management to Organization to Society to Selves.*

practitioners, and beyond recognizing them all as skills of growing demand since the report was published and until today, nothing speaks against the same skills being in demand also in the forthcoming decade. Those are as follows:

- ***Sensemaking:*** *the ability to determine the deeper meaning or significance of what is being expressed*
- ***Social intelligence:*** *the ability to connect to others in a deep and direct way, to sense and stimulate reactions and desired interactions*
- ***Novel & adaptive thinking:*** *proficiency at thinking and coming up with solutions and responses beyond that which is rote or rule based*
- ***Cross-cultural competency:*** *the ability to operate in different cultural settings*
- ***Computational thinking:*** *the ability to translate vast amounts of data into abstract concepts and to understand data-based reasoning*
- ***New media literacy:*** *the ability to critically assess and develop content that uses new media forms and to leverage these media for persuasive communication*
- ***Transdisciplinarity:*** *literacy in and ability to understand concepts across multiple disciplines*
- ***Design mindset:*** *the ability to represent and develop tasks and work processes for desired outcomes*
- ***Cognitive load management:*** *the ability to discriminate and filter information for importance and to understand how to maximize cognitive functioning using a variety of tools and techniques*
- ***Virtual collaboration:*** *the ability to work productively, drive engagement, and demonstrate presence as a member of a virtual team*[38]

It seems like strategies inspired by design and enabled through design management are more relevant than ever as a resource to meet the skills and competencies needed to face the demands of tomorrow.

---

[38]A. Davies, D. Fidler and D. Gorbis. 2011. *Future Works Skills 2020* (Palo Alto, CA: Institute for the Future, University of Phoenix Research Institute).

Digitization Strategies: How Design Excellence Helps Build Meaningful Digital and Technological Experiences

The importance of understanding how our knowledge about perception and sensemaking influences whether our decisions of digitalization and the introduction of new technologies are good or bad is one of the keys to successfully undertaking organizational change today. Weick duly reminds us of exactly that,[39] as does Madsbjerg in his recent book about sensemaking,[40] but it doesn't necessarily make it much more obvious how meaningful digital and technological experiences in a real-life setting are built. We live and work in demanding times as far as technological advance is concerned. New technologies and – not least – new terminologies and buzzwords are introduced all the time, and have been for decades, so this is not entirely new. However, for someone who is not a born digital, it can be challenging to keep up, to take it all in. Obviously, all the knowledge one needs is out there and can be acquired; hence, the actual challenge lies in formulating the overriding digital strategies and in knowing which expertise to hire or buy. To do so, a certain level of understanding needs to be present, although not necessarily in detail. This assumption is supported by the PwC report mapping the CEO challenges we've chosen to take as our point of departure. The gist of the challenge for today's leaders is not choosing the right software or systems but, on a much more transversal note, to handle the strategic and cultural effects of digitization:

> *CEOs are operating in a radically new environment. So how can they address the risks of globalization and technology, and realize the benefits for everyone?*[41]

---

[39]K.E. Weick. 1995. *Sensemaking in Organizations* (New York, NY: Sage Publications).
[40]C. Madsbjerg. 2017. *Sensemaking; What Makes Human Intelligence Essential in the Age of the Algorithm* (London: Little Brown Book Group).
[41]PwC. 2017. *20th CEO Survey: 20 years inside the mind of the CEO... What's next?* (London, UK: PwC), p. 13.

According to experts on the complexity of building a digital strategy, there are eight proven factors influencing the success of strategic information systems:

1. ***External, not internal, focus***
2. ***Adding value – not cost reduction***
3. ***Sharing the benefits***
4. ***Understanding customers and what they do with the product or service***
5. ***Business-driven, not technology-driven, innovation***
6. ***Incremental development, not the total application vision turned into reality***
7. ***Using the information gained from the systems to develop the business***
8. ***Monetizing information***[42]

What the eight factors boil down to is that technology, more than anything else, is an enabler of business development and competitiveness. In building meaningful digital and technological strategies – and experiences –more important than understanding the technology itself is to understand the environment in which the business operates: the value chain and all its players, behaviors, needs, and aspirations of the market and the inherent value of the knowledge and insights that is accumulated through each and every single digital transaction made.

To achieve this, it is axiomatic that the resources needed to build and develop a well-functioning digital infrastructure need to be in place. However, it is increasingly important is that the resources needed to build and develop a well-functioning mechanism to undertake user studies, engage stakeholders, and prototype the future are also there. One approach could be to create a "lab" to explore the ways in which the organization could possibly benefit from digitization and new technologies in the future.

The concept of creating intentional spaces and focusing resources toward experimentation, discovery, and innovation, has, over time,

---

[42]J. Peppard and J. Ward. 2016. *The Strategic Management of Information Systems: Building a Digital Strategy* (New York, NY: Wiley).

> *demonstrated the relevance of Labs for invention and development, scientific advancement, medical research and new technologies, as well as the emerging application toward solving complex societal challenges.*[43]

Such labs are not in their nature significantly different from what we often think about when hearing the word, namely, environments with scientists searching for revolutionary treatments or hitherto unknown chemical agents:

> *Similar to traditional science labs where the scientific method dictates the iterative process by which results are achieved, the newer class of Labs offers a neutral space dedicated to problem-solving in a highly experimental environment. Labs of this nature are sometimes referred to as innovation, change or design Labs.*[44]

The idea of labs and of prototyping the future is inspired by the way that designers have worked for more than a century. What has been added over the last couple of decades is a series of techniques and tools – tangible as well as digital – that facilitate the engagement of stakeholders and the way that information is sourced and processed. However, to benefit fully from a "future lab," it's not enough to dedicate a physical space, decorate it differently from the rest of the work environment, and allow for free play. A survey conducted by global consultant Cap Gemini Consulting showed that by 2015 38 percent of the world's 200 largest companies by revenue, across sectors, had set up innovation centers.[45] However, setting up an innovation lab – or future lab or whatever label you may choose to attach to it – is in itself no guarantee that all your qualms about the future will be laid to rest. In another survey from Cap Gemini, this time

---

[43]A.C. Rodrigues, J. Cubista and R. Simonsen. 2014. *Pototyping our Future* (Karlskrona, Sweden: Blekinge Institute of Technology).

[44]L. Torjman. 2012. *Labs: Designing the Future* (Toronto, ON, Canada: MaRS Discovery District).

[45]Capgemini Consulting & Altimeter. 2015. *The Innovation Game: Why and How Businesses Are Investing in Innovation Centers* (San Francisco, CA: Capgemini Consulting & Altimeter).

focusing on German companies, the experiences of 21 companies that have all established such units show that they all find such a unit valuable, they all see it as a continuous lèarning process, and they also recognize that there are issues to be resolved. The three most commonly mentioned concerns were as follows:

Lack of commitment and resources from mother company
Poor start-up and idea assessment

and

Low level of alignment and intensity of collaboration with mother company.[46]

Regardless of which approach is chosen to forecast the future and stay on top of digital and technological developments, there will be a need for processes that interpret all the knowledge produced and gathered into tangible value propositions. Design is one such mechanism, and if the objective is to identify where and how new technologies will serve at its best – whether externally, in the form of new products or services or internally, as levers of organizational development and improved processes – design needs to be applied both as a mindset and as a tool for exploration, framing, and reframing, and as a skill and a creative strategy to deliver profitable, viable, and meaningful solutions.

Strategies for Competitive Advantage: How Design Excellence Helps Your Organization Strengthen Its Competitiveness

In his book *Design-Driven Innovation,*, which discusses design's role and aptitude as driver of radical change and what things mean, Roberto Verganti writes in the introduction that

This strategy is called 'design-driven innovation' because design, in its etymological sense means 'making sense of things'. And design-driven

[46]Capgemini Consulting. 2016. *Insights into the German Landscape of Corporate Innovation Centers* (San Francisco, CA: Capgemini Consulting & Altimeter).

> *innovation is the R&D process for meanings. This book shows how companies can manage this process to radically overturn dominant meanings in an industry before their competitors do and therefore rule the competition.*[47]

There are several other takes on what "design driven" implies, but there is a particularly interesting twist to Verganti's approach, namely, the fundamental assumption that design is primarily about designing meaning, about sensemaking, and that these are the dominant components of strengthening competitiveness. Design can clearly contribute to making sense of products and services, as well as to creating new products and services through the conception of new meaning. Both require an intimate understanding of what the users are longing for, what makes them react and respond. This understanding can be acquired only through meaningful engagement of stakeholders and through access to tacit needs and aspirations. As Jon Kolko puts it in his book,

> *Design is more of a comprehensive way to think about people and human behaviour rather than engineering or marketing. It is a product development process that uses empathy with a community of potential consumers in order to identify problems to solve. Design leverages a certain way of thinking in order to infer solutions to those problems that will have meaningful emotional appeal and a strong market fit.*[48]

Design thinking is often portrayed as an approach to problem solving, while its much more pivotal role of informing and inspiring a deep and thorough understanding of the problem to be addressed is often forgotten. Solving the wrong problem – no matter how smartly it is solved – hardly strengthens any organization's competitiveness. Likewise, solving a problem in a designerly fashion – even one that is well conceived and rooted

---

[47] R. Verganti. 2009. *Design-Driven Innovation: Changing the Rules of Competition by Radically Innovating What Things Mean* (Boston, MA: Harvard Business Press).

[48] J. Kolko. 2014. *Well-Designed: How to Use Empathy to Create Products People Love* (Boston, MA: Harvard Business Review Press).

in real needs – only reflects positively through strengthened competitiveness if it's managed effectively and efficiently. Adopting design as a means to capture market shares and achieving a competitive edge is worthwhile only if design is allowed to play a role – not only as a means to solve any given problem, but also as a research instrument, a source of inspiration, and a means to manage the development process from the fuzziest notions to the successful launch of a new product, service, or proposition.

Competitiveness can be composed of many factors, but there is no doubt that understanding user needs is one of the most (if not *the* most) important requisites. However, the key to acquiring such an understanding is not always evident. In the design toolbox, a series of proven techniques contribute to accessing both the articulate and the tacit needs of the users; the author of *E-commerce Usability: Tools and techniques to perfect the on-line experience,* Dr. David Travis, at the website of the London-based consultancy "Userfocus," of which he is a partner, lists no less than 60 ways to understand user needs.[49] Most of them are either formally articulated or intrinsically part of the methodologies that design practitioners apply on a daily basis. That doesn't make them "design thinking" per se, but applied systematically as part of a project's front-end research, they inform and inspire the decisions to be made before an actual development project is embarked on.

Design management contributes to strengthening competitiveness through sustained focus on the findings from the user studies, recurring consultations, and consistent exploration of the ideas generated on their basis *throughout* the phases following the research and exploration phase, through to delivery. But also understanding the context in which a new product, service, or business model would exist is of pivotal importance. Porter's ***Five Forces***[50] – competitive rivalry, supplier power, buyer power, threat of substitution, and threat of new entry – can all be addressed and understood through design excellence. Embarking on any commercial design venture, a certain degree of analysis needs to precede. Other

---

[49]D. Tavis. 2014. "60 Ways to Understand User Needs that Aren't Focus Groups or Surveys." http://www.userfocus.co.uk/articles/60-ways-to-understand-user-needs.html.

[50]M.E. Porter. May 1979. "How Competitive Forces Shape Strategy," *Harvard Business Review* 59, no. 2, pp. 137-45.

techniques and approaches to this exist in addition to the Five Forces model, such as SWOT and PESTEL. All these three analyses or versions of them are very common, either alone or in combination. The objective of undertaking such analyses is to better understand the environment and conditions where a new product or service would potentially compete and the extent to which it would have a competitive advantage. Regardless of which of the aforementioned models or techniques are chosen, the core of the operation is to frame and forecast the critical factors influencing its competitiveness. The most effective approach to this is also a key element in design excellence: working with scenarios.

> *Scenario thinking offers a way for individuals and groups to face up to the threats and opportunities of the future, and their potential impact upon the organization or community.*[51]

> *Scenarios do not recast or reshape the present; rather they provide distinctive vantage points from which to re-examine, how the marketplace or industry is unfolding, which forces are shaping its evolution, and why it might evolve one way rather than another (Fahey, 2003).*[52]

While Porter focuses primarily on external factors to assess future competitiveness, Hamel and Prahalad are more occupied with the organization itself. Their thinking is based on the fundamental assumption that today's competitiveness is not something one can presume will continue in the future: "There's no such thing as 'sustaining' leadership; it must be regenerated again and again."[53] This argument is strongly supported by numerous later studies. One of the determining factors of whether an organization and its leadership succeed at "regenerating again and again"

---

[51]G. Wright and G. Cairns. 2011. *Scenario Thinking* (London, UK: Palgrave Macmillan).

[52]R. Cooper. S. Junginger, and T. Lockwood. 2009. *Design 2020 Design Industry Futures* (University of Salford, University of Lancaster and British Design Innovation).

[53]G. Hamel and C.K. Prahalad. 1994. *Competing for the Future*, Harvard Business Review, July-August 1994, adapted from the book *Competing for the Future*, published by Harvard Business School Press in September 1994.

boils down to their ability to deal with complexity, as complexity is conditional, not a matter of choice;

> *Leadership in these circumstances requires a broad mindset that is comfortable with complexity and ambiguity. It also requires a range of discrete skills that can support this mindset and are amenable to being refined through tried and tested development interventions: the ability to be flexible and responsive to change, the ability to find creative, innovative and original ways of solving problems, the ability to learn from mistakes, the ability to balance shorter and longer-term considerations.*[54]

One of the more famous quotes by the renowned authority on organizational culture, Edgar Schein;

> *In an increasingly complex, interdependent, and culturally diverse world, we cannot hope to understand and work with people from different occupational, professional, and national cultures if we do not know how to ask questions and build relationships.*[55]

It seems increasingly obvious that design excellence, hallmarked by the acknowledgment of ambiguity, questions and doubts, reiterations, and mistakes as drivers of better and more sustainable solutions, could be one of the levers most readily available to facilitate and accommodate the organizational development needed to stay competitive under constantly changing yet inevitably and increasingly complex conditions.

Improving Customer Experiences through Design Excellence

The final concern from the CEO panel was how to strengthen the organization's ability to deliver better customer experiences. This concern

---

[54]M. Gitsham. 2009. *Developing the Global Leader of Tomorrow*, Ashridge and EABIS.

[55]E. Schein. 2013. *Humble Inquiry: The Gentle Art of Asking Instead of Tellin* (San Francisco, CA: Berrett-Koehler Publishers).

cannot be discussed as a stand-alone, even less so than any of the preceding four.

> *Almost every successful company recognizes that it is in the business of customer experience. Many businesses understand that it's no longer enough to compete on products and services; how a company delivers for its customers is beginning to be as important as what it delivers. Customers - whether they're airline passengers, online retail consumers, or IT-services outsourcers - not only increasingly dictate the rules but also expect high levels of satisfaction from the savviest practitioners and the sleepiest industry participants alike. Companies that work to master this dynamic become superior competitors.*[56]

The perceived quality of the interaction between a company and its client – whether an individual or another company or organization – determines the degree of success that the company has. That sounds quite simple, and it would be if it weren't for variables like expectations and previous experience. Moreover, the combination of factors influences our perception:

> *The main findings include the notion that a factor can have a different impact on customer satisfaction and efficiency depending on which other factors it is combined with. Additionally, separate factors or the same factors in a different form influence customer satisfaction and efficiency. Hence, there are tradeoffs while attempting to achieve very good levels of both customer satisfaction and efficiency.*[57]

Studies show that "[o]ffering wonderful products and excellent service are hygiene factors today and do not lead to competitive advantage."[58]

---

[56]McKinsey & Company. 2016. *Customer Experience: Creating Value through Transforming Customer Journeys* (New York, NY: McKinsey & Company)

[57]T. Rekilä. *A Study of the Factors Influencing Customer Satisfaction and Efficiency in Contact Centers: The Combined Effect* [Master Thesis]. Espoo, Finland: Aalto University; 2013.

[58]F. Lemke, H. Wilson and M. Clark. 2014. *What Makes a Great Customer Experience?* (Cranfield, UK: Cranfield University, School of Management).

This only confirms Pine and Gilmore's studies of consumer economic trends, showing that the behavior of consumers was increasingly motivated by the quality of the experience as an equally important parameter to the quality of the service or good itself.[59] And, as if that weren't enough, there are significant differences between what triggers customer satisfaction in a B2B as opposed to a B2G or B2C transaction. Other studies support this, and also confirm the notion that clients and customers weigh different factors differently but that to succeed companies "will have to be capable of achieving high experience quality levels consistently across all channels."[60] Some years ago, KPMG published a seven-step guide to improved customer experience:

1. ***Understand the needs, wants, and preferences of your target audience***
2. ***Establish economic frameworks to understand and prioritize impact of marketing, sales, and service decisions***
3. ***Track customer behavior, distill patterns, and adapt to accommodate shifts***
4. ***Develop lead nurturing and customer management plans for target audiences***
5. ***Develop a customer-centric information architecture***
6. ***Deploy workflow-based tools to marketing, sales, and service stakeholder groups***
7. ***Create a customer experience map to optimize touch points***[61]

Among the interesting observations here is that the seven steps in many ways resemble and correspond to the sequences known from design management, while the contents greatly correspond to the exploration, insights, and inspiration one would normally connote to design thinking,

---

[59]J. Pine and J. Gilmore. 1999. *The Experience Economy* (Boston, MA: Harvard Business School Press).

[60]F. Lemke, H. Wilson and M. Clark. 2014. *What Makes a Great Customer Experience?* (Cranfield, UK: Cranfield University, School of Management).

[61]KPMG. 2011. *Seven Steps to Better Customer Experience Management: Improving Customer Management to Drive Profitable Growth* (Amstelveen, Netherlands: KPMG).

supporting the argument that design excellence is a viable approach to understanding current and improving future customer experiences.

Designers are not only trained in but also work systematically with understanding needs, wants, and preferences; prioritizing alternative routes of impact; tracking customer behavior; and distilling patterns, with diverse target audiences, with customer-centric information architecture, with engaging multiple stakeholders, and with touchpoints and user journeys – here referred to as experience maps. At its core, what KPMG recommends is a properly conceived and professionally managed design process to " drive growth and profitability using customer experience as a service differentiator."[62] Some would call it user experience design, others service design; what it adds up to is that the process of getting to the point where the perceived experience supports the brand values, the strategies, and the aspirations of the provider of the experience – whether it includes a physical product or a service transaction – by being perceived as superior to that of its competitors by its clients is a design process:

> *While colloquially the word design is used to refer to the appearance or styling of a particular product or outcome, the proper meaning goes far beyond that. In particular, the approach of service design refers to the process of designing rather than its outcome. The outcome of a service design process can have various forms: rather abstract organizational structures, operation processes, service experiences and even concrete physical objects.*[63]

Design as Making Your Business Tangible

Traditionally, design processes result in tangible outputs, tangible as in something material that can be touched and felt. As design, as previously discussed, captured new intangible domains, such as services and

[62]KPMG. 2011. *Seven Steps to Better Customer Experience Management: Improving Customer Management to Drive Profitable Growth* (Amstelveen, Netherlands: KPMG).

[63]M. Stickdorn and J. Schneider. 2011. *This is Service Design Thinking* (Amsterdam: BIS Publishing).

experiences, the role of, and interest in, immaterial design emerged and matured.

> *The solutions to the "wicked problems of design" are more likely to be new processes, lifestyles, and changes in meaning, rather than purely material artefacts.*[64]

Yet one of the key roles of design and designers is to make the intangible tangible – often through visualizations – but

> *The notion of bringing form to the intangible complex not only refers to visual modes of representation but also includes narrative practices and storytelling as an art.*[65]

This view is widely supported:

> *Examples of new application areas for knowledge visualization can be found, for example, in the visual communication of corporate missions, strategies, value propositions, and business scenarios. New applications can also be envisioned by combining knowledge visualization with other innovative approaches in knowledge management, such as storytelling.*[66]

Many of us have experienced how powerful it is when a visual facilitator captures a conference or strategy meeting. Our understanding of complex issues and not already existing solutions is significantly improved by seeing visual representations of it. Also, three-dimensional props

---

[64]D.C. Wahl and S. Baxter. Spring 2008. "The Designer's Role in Facilitating Sustainable Solutions," *MIT* 24, no. 2.

[65]B. Dixon and E. Murphy. 2016. "Educating for Appropriate Design Practice: Insights from Design Innovation," *Design Management Journal* 11, pp. 58-66. doi:10.1111/dmj.12027.

[66]M.J. Eppler and R.A. Burkhard. 2007. "Visual Representations in Knowledge Management: Framework and Cases," *Journal of Knowledge Management* 11, no. 4, pp. 112-22.

underpin our intellectual processing. An example of such is LEGO Serious Play (LSP), which is a process developed to support strategic dialogue and processes. Extensive research has been undertaken to understand how serious play enhances strategy processes. One research project showed that LSP helped motivate the workshop members, helped participants see their ideas or suggestions integrated in the overall solution, enhanced the communication of the workshop results, allowed for a guided discussion as well as creativity, and strengthened the consensus around the gathered options for action.[67] Other elements of the design process, such as continuous prototyping, have been adopted, first by the software and programming communities, and later on by numerous others devoted to the development of private and public services, urban planning, new business models and disruptive challengers within all kinds of industries, in the form and shape of "hackathons."

> *Hackathon combines the terms "hacking" and "marathon" and implies an intense, uninterrupted, period of programming. More specifically, a hackathon is a highly engaging, continuous event in which people in small groups produce a working software prototype in a limited amount of time.*[68]

And, as mentioned before, not only software and user interfaces, but any conceivable material or immaterial outcome. The point is that tools and methods, previously known predominantly from the design domain, have already been taken up by other sectors on a massive scale to generate ideas and moderate stakeholder conversations, prototyping and making tangible. Design is all about making tangible; making ideas work and bringing ingenuity to life. What remains to be seen is that the mechanisms proven to manage and extract the most value out of such tools and

---

[67]V. Grienitz and A.M. Schmidt. 2012. "Scenario Workshops for Strategic Management with Lego Serious Play," *Problems of Management in the 21st Century*, 3, pp. 26-36.

[68]M. Raatikainen, M. Komssi, V. dal Bianco, K. Kindstöm and J. Järvinen. 2013. *Industrial Experiences of Organizing a Hackathon to Assess a Device-Centric Cloud Ecosystem*, Proc. 2013 Computer Software and Applications Conf., pp. 790-799.

methods – design management – are adopted to the same degree and as widely as the individual elements referred to. As stated earlier, design thinking seems to have captured the minds and attention of both the private and public sectors, whereas design management in the wake of this new, or rather newly rediscovered and widely perceived "one size fits all" remedy – proverbially spoken – was thrown out with the bathwater.

PART 5

Design thinking, primarily, is an approach and strategic framework to rethink an organization's products and services, value chains and business models, as well as visions and readiness for change and innovation. Design management is, primarily, the coordination of the means and methods, the skills and capabilities, as well as the allocation of the resources necessary to deal with the complexity of the design process, on an operational, tactical, and strategic level.

Design Management Excellence

The way that a discussion evolves over time depends, to a certain degree, on who defines the agenda. As for the quite dramatic evolution that design has been through during the last two decades, in particular, the agenda has been set by everyone but designers. Clearly, scholars from various backgrounds with an interest in design have influenced the discourse through papers and books and conferences, but as the role of design was slowly latched onto topics such as growth, innovation, and competitiveness, it also captured the interest of policy makers and bureaucrats. Although design previously appeared to be somewhat factional and of little interest in terms of economic growth and prosperity, by latching design onto strategy as a vehicle, it was suddenly perceived as an instrument with other qualities than before.

Mapping Design in Organizations as Aesthetics in Organization Theory

Veiled by the enthusiasm of the how design could coexist with, be inspired by, and enhance strategic objectives, some of the core qualities of design – such as aesthetics and tactility and the importance of appearance – seemed to be somewhat oppressed. For quite some time during the first decade of the century, opening a discussion on design and aesthetics most often elicited condescending comments, indicating that design had moved on from there a long time ago.

More recently, the acknowledgment of the role of aesthetics as a strategically important factor has made it possible to discuss design as a much more diverse and multifaceted concept, containing both tangible and measurable as well as less palpable qualities. A former Danish minister of culture once said that

> *Meaning can never come from rationality only. Rationality can show us the easiest way to a goal, but it can never tell us how to get there, where we are going. That's why art and architecture are important to our world.*[1]

Just as there was little room for aesthetics during the hype of strategic design, design management lost out to the far catchier design thinking a decade later. Whereas the concept of design management never really penetrated the membrane between the design research community and the real world, the concept of design thinking resonated with a number of agendas. One of its advocates, *Business Week* editor Bruce Nussbaum, had little doubt:

> *I now believe that CEOs and managers must know Design Thinking to do their jobs. CEOs must be designers and use their methodologies to actually run companies. Let me be even more precise. Design Thinking is the new Management Methodology.*[2]

---

[1]M. Jelved. 2014. From inaugural speech at the Venice Biennale in 2014, where the title of the Danish pavilion was "Empowerment of Aesthetics."

[2]B. Nussbaum. 2007. "CEOs Must Be Designers, Not Just Hire Them. Think Steve Jobs and iPhone," *The Economist*, June 28, 2007.

Less than 4 years later, he diagnosed that

Design Thinking has given the design profession and society at large all the benefits it has to offer and is beginning to ossify and actually do harm.[3]

A number of things indicate that he was first right and then wrong. Design thinking wasn't dead at all. It has changed and matured, and it still takes on different masks, but the number of conferences and publications about design thinking is increasing, and the number of domains in which it is embraced and applied is constantly growing and increasingly diverse (Figure 8).

PERIOD	1965 -1992	1993-2005	2005-2014	2015 -1017
DM adds value through ...	Economic value (Aesthetics. Differerenta-tion) Product value (Quality) Perception value	Process value Innovation (Coordination. Problem solving)	Human value (Human and cultural value transformation)	Strategic conver-sation (Building skills Framing probtems)
DM solves design problems relating to ...	All aspects of the company's artifacts	Managing Innovation	Strategic diagnosis Changes in society, in politics	Cultural changes Digital transfor-mation Design for all
DM develops and fuels design skills in the functions of ...	Direction Marketing Operations Communications	R&O Interdisciplinary innovation team	Finance Human resources	Every function in the company
Design leadership (design dire-ction. artistic direction) helps the accomplishment of goals such as ...	Create a brand and an identity (coherence between design disciplines) Create profit for the company	Ceate new products and services Improve the innovation process and its efficiency	Make companies aware of design strategy Change for customer oriented and creative culture	Make a company sustainable in a globalized con-text of societal wellbeing

Figure 8 Half a Century of Design Management and Design Thinking
Source: Borja de Mozota. 2018. Half a Century of Design Management and Design Thinking.

[3]B. Nussbaum. 2011. *Design Thinking Is a Failed Experiment. So, What's Next?* CO.DESIGN, May 4, 2011.

Design thinking seems to be here to stay –at least for a while –although some may argue that it suffers from the lack of a precise and unambiguous definition, whereas others see this as one of its unique assets.

Design Thinking in Business Education

Although not necessarily helping us define the concept, one approach to forecasting its future role, thus framing it from a bottom-up perspective, might be to map how it is dealt with in higher education. One recent study showed that

> *Many universities were found to have programs where students were exposed to design thinking in classroom situations and workshops around problem-based issues. From the review of all data, four areas of categorization emerged; (i) Human Centered Design; (ii) Integrative Thinking, (iii) Design Management, and (iv) Design as Strategy.*[4]

Design thinking is conceived as encompassing the principles of ***Human-Centered Design***; an emphatic approach to the people involved in or affected by a novelty or change, duly considering human needs, desires, and intuition.

> *Today's human centered design is based on the use of techniques which communicate, interact, empathize and stimulate the people involved, obtaining an understanding of their needs, desires and experiences which often transcends that which the people themselves actually realized. Practiced in its most basic form, human centred design leads to products, systems and services which are physically, perceptually, cognitively and emotionally intuitive.*[5]

---

[4]J. Matthews and C. Wrigley. 2017. "Design and Design Thinking in Business and Management Higher Education," *Journal of Learning Design* 10, no. 1.

[5]J. Giacomin. 2014. "What Is Human Centred Design?" *Design Journal* 17, no. 4, pp. 606-23.

Furthermore, the concept encompasses ***Integrative Thinking***, fronted, among others, by Roger Martin. He frames the concept by describing the core of how integrative thinkers work:

> *Integrative thinkers work to see the whole problem, embrace its multi-varied nature, and understand the complexity of its causal relationships.*[6]

And, latching it onto design thinking,

> *Rather than perpetuating the past, the design thinker creates the future.*[7]

Whether one prefers integrative thinking or systemic thinking, which seems to be referred to more often today, there is a fundamental notion that no problem or challenge exists in isolation, and that solving it – not for its own good sake, but as a piece of the puzzle that creates the future – requires an understanding of its context and cause. Then, interestingly enough, ***Design Management*** appears to be conceived as an integral element in design thinking. According to Design Management Institute (DMI),

> *Design management encompasses the on-going processes, business decisions, and strategies that enable innovation and create effectively designed products, services, communications, environments, and brands that enhance our quality of life and provide organizational success. On a deeper level, design management seeks to link design, innovation, technology, management and customers to provide competitive advantage across the triple bottom line: economic, social/cultural, and environmental factors. It is the art and science of empowering design*

---

[6]R. Martin. Fall 1999. *The Art of Integrative Thinking* (Toronto, ON, Canada: Rotman Management).

[7]R. Martin. 2009. *The Design of Business – Why Design Thinking Is the Next Competitive Advantage* (Boston, MA: Harvard Business Press).

to enhance collaboration and synergy between "design" and "business" to improve design effectiveness.[8]

Whereas the first component focuses on the engagement in actual design activities and on undertaking the activities needed to understand the people involved and the second component focuses on the analysis of the challenge at hand, its cause and context, the third component focuses on the structures and processes needed to organize and take advantage of the skills and knowledge brought into the project. The final conceived component of design thinking is labeled ***Design as Strategy***.

Revisiting the Design Ladder previously referred to, which was developed at the very beginning of the century to measure the various stages of design engagement that organizations have, the highest level of engagement is design for strategy, which was elaborated on in a more recent article:

The designer works with the company's owners/management to rethink the business concept completely or in part. Here, the key focus is on the design process in relation to the company's business visions and its desired business areas and future role in the value chain.[9]

The most significant difference between this last component and the three former ones is that the first refers to the development of products, services, and systems – or to the integration and management of processes and structures – whereas the latter relates to the organization as a whole, to its visions, and overruling strategies.

Design offers a different approach and suggests processes that are more widely participative, more dialogue-based, issue-rather than calendar-driven, conflict -using rather than conflict-avoiding, all aimed at invention and learning, rather than control. If we were to

---

[8]www.dmi.org/?What_is_Design_Management

[9]Danish Design Centre. 2015. *The Design Ladder: Four Steps of Design Use* (Copenhagen: Danish Design Centre).

take design's lead, we would involve more members of the organization in two-way strategic conversations. We would view the process as one of iteration and experimentation and pay sequential attention to idea generation and evaluation in a way that attends first to possibilities before moving onto constraints.[10]

A challenge, however, might be to find accomplices. Not all managers have access to experienced designers, but actually reading about "successful stories of what works" can help a great deal, because managers desiring to use design thinking will often have to build their own set of skills – on their own.

We believe that inside the "black box" of design thinking is a process that managers can be taught. And that's because we are not talking about turning managers into designers but about helping them to become better design thinkers, literate in the tools and process that designers use and able to use that process, not to design their products but to solve their business problems.[11]

"Dancing with Hierarchies" (Mary Parker Follett 1868 to 1933)

Mary Parker Follett introduced the idea of power as a framework for mutual understanding, as an energy that emanated from the circular response between people and ideas, so that power was nonhierarchical in the sense that it was not "power over another person" but rather "joint power over the situation." Translating this into the relation between design, designers, and managers, it emphasizes the need for a circular understanding of the different roles and different contributions of design, design management, and design thinking.

---

[10]J. Liedtka. 2006. *If Managers Thought Like Designers;* Rotman Magazine Spring/ Summer 2006

[11]J. Liedtka, A. King and K. Bennet. 2013. *Solving Problems with Design Thinking: 10 Stories of What Works* (Columbia: Columbia Business School Publishing).

> *Organizations in order to take advantage of the specific competence of designers need to change their members' hierarchical thinking and notion of power.*[12]

A jointly developed power becomes coactive, and not coercive. For Follett, instead of trying to compete for power, the situation at hand – the one that we are in together – is turned into one characterized by joint ownership and joint aspiration. Hence, Follett's concept of power over the situation becomes an alternative to the competition and positioning often standing in the way of truly benefiting from design thinking in organizations. Follett sees the coactive power as what is needed for creative thinking and applied creativity to jointly develop integrative solutions. When "power with" is more important than "power over," potential conflicts can be handled creatively in order to find integrative solutions, rather than settling for nonideal compromises or submissiveness to the domination of one party. The design process is an iterative process, allowing for the paradoxical coexistence of chaos and structure and also fragmenting traditional hierarchical patterns, by seamlessly moving between holism and the attention to detail – and back again – building the capacity to both form and dissolve structures. Being able to apply a holistic approach is crucial to successful collaboration between designers and other groups, such as marketers, engineers, and the C-suite. Although designers rarely pretend to be experts in marketing or engineering, in order to work with them they need sufficient knowledge of the disciplines to understand their contribution to the whole. Such a relationship cannot be hierarchical, placing one discipline above the other. It depends on mutuality and collaboration within "the law of the situation," and power becomes the ability to make things happen … to initiate change.

According to Tom Kelley, taking advantage of designers' competences in applying empathy without dominance is to find new paths out of the

---

[12] U. Johansson and J. Woodilla. 2010. Collection 1, Design & Sociology - *Dancing with Hierarchies (Reprint Design Journal September 2008).*

hierarchical prison.[13] Others have reframed the concept of design thinking under other names, such as "design leadership":

> *Design leadership helps define the future – design management provides the tools for getting there.*[14]

yet without changing the gist of it all. However, if design thinking is both an approach to the development of products, services and systems, a mechanism to integrate and manage design into or alongside existing processes and structures, as well as a means of enhancing the strategic conversations in an organization – which seems almost all-encompassing – then what is design management that design thinking is not? There is no unequivocal answer to that question. Design can be practiced in ways that are inspired by management, just as management can be practiced in ways that are inspired by design. Strategic design management leans itself closely up against and requires the presence of design thinking, while design thinking quite unremarkably opens the door to strategic design management (Figure 9).

We just learned that design management is

> *...the art and science of empowering design to enhance collaboration and synergy between "design" and "business" to improve design effectiveness.*[15]

Moreover, according to Design Management Europe,

> *The concept of design management relates to certain management activities, methods and skills that are required to optimize and manage*

[13]T. Kelley. 2005. *The Ten Faces of Innovation: IDEO's Strategies for Beating the Devil's Advocate and Driving Creativity Throughout Your Organization* (New York, NY: Doubleday).

[14]R. Turner. 2013. *Design Leadership: Securing the Strategic Value of Design* (London, UK: Gower Publishing).

[15]www.dmi.org/?What_is_Design_Management

	DM ▶	DM	◀ dM
Product and service strategy	Design reinforces user orientation (market research, aesthetic value, brand) ▶	"Good design" Beauty in utility	◀ Management reinforces the efficiency of design management in the offer and the brand
Innovation strategy	Design reinforces collaboration between participants (forces systems thinking) ▶	Process design Co-design Inclusive design	◀ Management reinforces the credibility of design with the management tools of the design function
Human resources strategy	Design changes company culture (more creative) and people's autonomy (creativity) ▶	UX Design Design thinking	◀ Management reinforces the pertinence of the design strategy by managing coordination with HR
Company strategy	Design changes the vision between the company and its environment (prospective, research) ▶	Design strategy	◀ Management reinforces the credibility of the design function by implementing performance indicators
Strategic audit	Design opens a prospective conversation between the company and its environment ▶	Critical design Concept design	◀ Management reinforces the credibility of design with the support of senior management (research, experimentation)

PROBLEMS

- The issue of measuring the value of client satisfaction and brand value (perception)
- The issue of thinking company and not only "products"
- The issue of the company's materiality
- The issue of systems thinking in the structure
- The issue of contextual design projects versus standard management norms

D=Design, M= Manegement

Figure 9 The Two Forces of Design Management and Strategic Design

Source: Borja de Mozota. 2018. The Two Forces of Design Management and Strategic Design.

design processes. This is dictated by the highly complex nature of the design process.[16]

[16]G.L. Koostra. 2009. *The Incorporation of Design Management in Today's Business Practices: An Analysis of Design Management Practices in Europe*, DME Survey 2009, Design Management Europe.

Still keeping in mind Raymond Turner's definition, namely, that design management provides the tools to getting to a future conceived through design leadership, and adding two more aspects on design thinking and design management from two of the scholars who have also been deeply engaged in the practice of both,

> *Design thinking is essentially a human-centered innovation process that emphasizes observation, collaboration, fast learning, and visualization of ideas, rapid concept prototyping, and concurrent business analysis, which ultimately influences innovation and business strategy.*[17]

and

> *Today the language of design management is changing – and design leadership is the new mantra instead of strategic design management. Design management is used to describe what we in the past called design project management, while the term design leadership is used to describe a more strategic level related to the vision for how design could be used within an organisation to achieve corporate goals.*[18]

The "hierarchy" of design is portrayed in Ralf Beuker's model (Figure 10) of design and its relatives, depicting the degree of organizational impact as well as the degree of abstraction in thinking. Design only rarely greatly influences overall organizational strategies and is often focused on a fairly tangible output – even when not literally so. Design management has, as it relates to skills, methods, and capabilities, as well as structures and processes, noticeably more influence on the organization as such and implies numerous operations on a rather abstract level, while design thinking per se is rather abstract, but with a significant degree of influence on overriding strategies and visions for the organization. Revisiting the introductory chapter of this book, we argued that

---

[17]T. Lockwood. 2009. *Design Thinking: Integrating Innovation, Customer Experience, and Brand Value* (New York, NY: Allworth).

[18]J. Gloppen. 2008. Perspectives on design leadership and design thinking in the service industry. *International DMI Education Conference*, April 14-15, 2008, ESSEC Business School, Cergy-Pointoise, France.

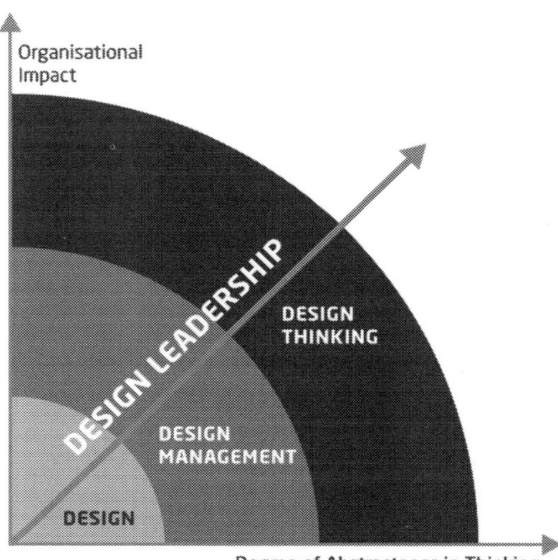

Figure 10 R. Beuker. 2011: Design and its Relatives
Source: Beuker. 2011. Keynote, 1st Cambridge Design Management Conference.

> *..., a more recent approach to design management is to consider it as a means of enhancing the ability of an organization to take up new knowledge and embrace creativity on a strategic level and as an integrated element of organizational or corporate culture, revealing its commonalities with concepts like design thinking and the emerging discipline of organizational design.*

That point of view still seems to hold.

Building the Convergence between Design Leadership and Design Management

From this, one could deduce that *design thinking* – **primarily** – is an approach and a strategic framework to rethink an organization's products and services, value chains, and business models, as well as visions and readiness for change and innovation. Design management is – **primarily** – the coordination of the means and methods, the skills and capabilities, as well as the allocation of the resources necessary to deal with the complexity of the design process, on an operational, tactical, and strategic level. Hence, design management and design thinking are related on many levels and, despite originating in different scholarly environments, converg with regard to core findings and derived evidence. And yet they are neither synonymous nor interchangeable – for at least four very good reasons:

 # 1: *Design Management is the common space for managers and designers; design thinking is the common space for leadership and design*
 # 2: *Design Thinking is – at worst – meaningless if it's not firmly vested in and endorsed by senior management; design management can add value also when applied on managerial levels*
 # 3: *Design Management requires process coordination and optimization skills, whereas design thinking requires visionary leadership*
 # 4: *Design Thinking provides the vision and leadership (empowers); design management the business case (enables)*

Crucial Difference # 1

Design management is the common space for managers and designers; design thinking for leadership and design.

We have already argued the role of the gap between design and business and their respective, and notoriously different, worldviews. The extent to which these are vested in real differences as opposed to perception based on reciprocal biases is not for us to say, but the existence of both seems to be a mere fact. However, instead of dwelling on the differences, we believe in searching for common ground: spaces where the two meet are needed for the realization of the potential of both domains. The underestimated value of design as such was already very clearly articulated by Kotler and Rath in 1984:

Design is a potent strategic tool that companies can use to gain a sustainable competitive advantage. Yet most companies neglect design as a strategy tool. What they don't realize is that good design can enhance products, environment, communications, and corporate identity.[19]

And, quite clearly, since then – over a period of more than 30 years – the proliferation of design has increased steadily, so much so that a survey from 2016 showed that 58 percent of companies with more than 10 employees in Denmark use design, which is a distinct, though not surprisingly massive, improvement from 2003, where a comparable analysis in Denmark showed that 48.9 percent used design.[20,21]

What seems more surprising in light of the attention given to design – not only as a means to "enhance products, environment, communications, and corporate identity" but also as an approach to business development, which has proven its transversal value across all conceivable sectors – is that of the companies asked, which do not consciously use design, 86 percent do not see design as "relevant for them or their line of business." This is especially so in light of the quite extensive investments in design promotion and governmental support in all industrialized countries, even though the financial investments in such activities are not easily accounted for.

The general assumption, however, is that "[t]oday, practically all developed countries have some national initiatives in support of design, although with varying levels of maturity."[22]

Although one might have thought that decades of European, national, regional, and local design support and promotion programs would have brought about a more significant change of behavior and attitude vis-à-vis the role and value creation of design, there is still a long way to go.

And although design is still considered to be of marginal or no importance at all by a rather significant portion of private sector organizations in Europe – as well as by public sector, without having been able to find

---

[19] P. Kotler and G. Alexander Rath. 1984. "Design: A Powerful but Neglected Strategic Tool," *Journal of Business Strategy* 5, no. 2.

[20] Danish Design Centre and Federation of Danish Industries. 2017. *Design Delivers* (Copenhagen: Danish Design Centre and Federation of Danish Industries).

[21] National Agency for Enterprise and Housing. 2003. *The Economic Effects of Design.*

[22] EU Commission. 2009. *Commission Staff Working Document: Design as a Driver of User-Centred Innovation* (Brussels, Belgium: EU Commission), p. 32.

reliable figures to support it – it has somehow found a space in the collective consciousness of professionals, whether as a craft, as a means to give form and shape to products, or as a strategic tool, methodology, or mindset, as often referred to when the discussion enters the domain of design thinking. Design management, on the other hand, is still struggling with being unrecognized or unheard of by most, which to some extent is quite puzzling, as it leans itself up against one of the most commonly practiced management disciplines: project management – albeit with exclusive focus on delivering on design processes and building design awareness and capacity within an organization.

Thus, design management as a common space for managers and designers and a key to a more constructive conversation between design managers and their colleagues with merely a different point of departure could be worth a closer look. In her book on design management, design researcher, educator, and author Kathryn Best categorizes design management into three compartments, managing the design strategy, managing the design process, and managing the design implementation.[23] As such, design management differs little from other forms of project management, or management as such, for that matter;

> *Managing a project is like the management of any activity. Two fundamental steps are involved in such management, namely, the making and implementation of decisions. There is a substantial body of knowledge regarding how decisions can be made – in particular how to consider the evaluation of risk and uncertainty in the potential use of resources committed through the decision process.*[24]

Thus, one of the most obvious points of departure for this exploration would be to focus on the kinship between design managers and all of those with whom the design manager needs to collaborate closely.

A project manager may not be responsible for the development of strategies, or even the underlying strategy for the project or projects he

---

[23]K. Best. 2006. *Design Management: Managing Design Strategy, Process and Implementation* (Lausanne, Switzerland: AVA Publishing).

[24]D.I. Cleland. 2006. *Project Management: Strategic Design and Implementation* (New York, NY: McGraw-Hill), 5th ed.

or she is asked to manage. But a fundamental responsibility is to ensure that the project or projects – branches, if you wish – are managed in alignment with their strategic stem. The same is most certainly also the case for the design manager – whether the objective of the process is a new product or service to enhance an already existing range or spark a new business venture, or a new visual identity to reflect a brand promise, or a new user interface to support a novel business model, none of which makes any sense unless strategically embedded. Likewise, the choice of process and methodology, resources, and metrics throughout the project life cycle is the responsibility of the project manager, as is the choice of tools to be applied, stakeholders to be engaged, and prototyping techniques to be tapped into. Just as with any other process, those are choices not to be made lightly, as no strategy, no end goal, and no process leading thereto are ever exactly the same. The hallmark of good project management as well as design management is the effectiveness and smoothness with which the strategic goals are met or surpassed.

Implementation is often a sore point. While the conception and development of any new or improved solution is often seen as projects isolated within the confines of an R&D, innovation, or business development department – or something cooked up by the accounting, marketing, or HR departments – the implementation is the ultimate test of whether all relevant stakeholders have been engaged to the extent needed to embrace and give the novelty a chance. As pointed out earlier, there are seven proven psychological motives to resist change, ranging from fear, alienation, and infringement to guilt, focus on own needs, the feeling of being downright threatened, or plain and simple uncertainty. Unless all of those have been addressed throughout the development phases, implementation most certainly involves risks of being rejected or resisted, both being barriers to successful implementation. Hence, whether the new and unknown can be categorized as a design project or any other kind of project, the challenges, from the business case stage through to successful implementation, are very much the same, including what Porter claims to be one of the key activities when implementing a strategy: deciding what not to do.

> *Strategy is making trade-offs in competing. The essence of strategy is choosing what not to do. Positioning choices determine not only which*

activities a company will perform and how it will configure individual activities, but also how activities relate to one another. While operational effectiveness is about achieving excellence in individual activities and functions, strategy is about combining activities.[25]

One could start defining what goes into this common space for managers and designers and ask what they can learn from each other and how their joint endeavors can contribute to a better result, exploiting the kinship instead of looking for differences and what sets them apart. Practitioners and scholars from both sides would tend to support the view that most designers would benefit from strengthening their business acumen, while business managers would benefit from adapting a more "designerly"[26] approach to their projects. And, just as there is an easily identifiable convergence between the role of managers and that of designers, as seen through the lens of design management, the two concepts, design and leadership, are also closely related. Design – regardless of whether one leans against Simon's **"devising courses of action aimed at changing existing situations into preferred ones",**[27] Schön's **"explorative works,"**[28] or Visser's **"construction of representations"**[29] – and leadership, as we know it from the literature; a leader innovates, is an original, develops, focuses on people, inspires trust, has a long-term perspective, asks what and why, has an eye on the horizon, originates, challenges status quo, and does the right thing, as opposed to doing things right[30]; both revolve around creating something that doesn't already exist or around improving what does. Design and leadership are both about

---

[25]M. Porter. 1998. "What is Strategy?" In *The Strategy Reader*, ed. S. Segal-Horn. New York, NY: Basic Blackwell.

[26]N. Cross. 2007. *Designerly Ways of Knowing* (Basel, Switzerland: Birkenhauser Architecture).

[27]H.A. Simon. 1969. *The Sciences of the Artificial* (Boston, MA: MIT Press), 3rd Edition 1996

[28]D. Schön. 1983. *The Reflective Practitioner: How Professionals Think in Action* (New York, NY: Basic Books).

[29]W. Visser. 2006. "Designing as Construction of Representations: A Dynamic Viewpoint in Cognitive Design Research," *Human–Computer Interaction* 21, no. 1.

[30]W. Bennis. 1989. Extracted from and Condensed by the Authors: *On Becoming a Leader* (New York, NY: Addison Wesley).

vision and aspirations and about dreaming of the future, whereas the role of the designer and the manager is to materialize visions, to gather aspirational momentum, and to deliver on the dreams of the future. The bridge between the visions as interpreted through beyond state-of-the-art design solutions and the aspirations of great leaders as we know them from all walks of life, from companies, organizations and nations, is what we have come to know as design thinking – in all its shapes and shades. And the concept of leadership most certainly also includes thought leadership.

Design management and design thinking are domains where ***designers and managers, design and leadership play different yet closely related roles*** but are all fueled by the same energy and the same ideals and are fundamentally all vital forces in supporting the key elements of what Kaplan called the strategic management system: clarifying and translating vision and strategy, communicating and linking strategic objectives and measures, planning, setting targets and aligning strategic initiatives, and enhancing strategic feedback and learning, recognizing that

> *Balanced Scorecard is a management system that can channel the energies, abilities, and specific knowledge held by people throughout the organization toward achieving long-term strategic goals.*[31]

Hence, underpinning exactly the same objectives as those that design thinking and design management have proven to be invaluable.

Crucial Difference # 2

Design Thinking is – at worst – meaningless if it's not firmly vested in and endorsed by senior management; design management can add value also when applied on managerial levels.

For an organization to change its collective behavior, its ideas and its culture, leadership is needed, and an organization's journey toward new horizons without the endorsement of its ultimate decision makers will almost certainly be in vain. Design thinking has been commonly presented as a smarter way

---

[31] R.S. Kaplan and D.P. Norton. 1996. *The Balanced Scorecard: Translating Strategy into Action* (Boston, MA: Harvard Business Press).

of solving problems, of tapping into the creative capacity of an organization, and of achieving better results through user focus and engagement.

> *The value delivered by design thinking is almost always seen to be improvements in the creativity and usefulness of the solutions produced.*[32]

Our postulate would be that design thinking – although also used as a tool for "improvements in the creativity and usefulness of the solutions produced" – is not effectively exploited as something an organization applies on a project-to-project basis or a tool that is tucked away when the project is over. In reality, much of what is often referred to as design thinking would more fittingly be labeled design management. It can most certainly benefit all kinds of product and service development projects, but to be truly valuable, it requires depth and immersion. But although as powerful and effective a mechanism for change as it can be, it is also demanding, as in its slipstream comes transformation.

> *At its best, the design movement seeks to bring innovations – sometimes radical innovations – to organizations that have to adapt to new circumstances of economic competition, social expectation, and cultural understanding.*

Despite making this confident assertion, Richard Buchanan, in the same article, also admits to the doubts and to challenges yet to be met:

> *Can design shape organizational culture so that the organization positively affects the thought and behavior of individuals? The true test will be the degree to which our efforts to introduce design thinking into the management of organizations embodies the fundamental principle of design.*[33]

---

[32]J. Liedtka. 2017. Beyond better solutions: Design thinking as a social technology. *Conference Proceedings of the Design Management Academy Research Perspectives on Creative Intersections*, Hong Kong.

[33]R. Buchanan. 2015. "Worlds in the Making: Design, Management, and the Reform of Organizational Culture," *She Ji: The Journal of Design, Economics, and Innovation* 1, no. 1, pp. 5-21.

Are organizations truly prepared to immerse themselves in such a potentially powerful force for transformation, transformation that not only exacts design thinking, but that also requires what we call "systemic thinking"? This is a way of thinking that emphasizes connectedness and enables people to see the bigger picture, one in which owners, solvers, solutions, problem-solving methods, and problem descriptions are portrayed as a whole system.[34] Design thinking embodies this immense potential, but, again, only if it's truly embraced by an organization's senior management.

Design management is also powerful in its own right and can often be the forerunner to the adoption of design as a more transversal force in an organization while, in the meantime, it can also stand on its own feet from project to project. Studies have shown that the appreciation of design can successfully be built from the inside through the adoption of design in projects of limited scale and consequence and that companies with little or no prior design knowledge are better able to cope with designers and the challenges of absorbing new design knowledge if they themselves build design management capabilities.[35] However, while design management capacity can be acquired and benefited from in different ways, through procurement, either as a separate or as part of a combined service, or by the "Trojan Horse" approach, as just described, and in many other combinations of internal and external forces, design thinking *cannot* be procured as a service or delegated to an arbitrary internal department or team. Whereas design management can contribute to improved processes throughout and on any level in an organization, design thinking must be firmly vested in and endorsed at the very top of the organization, where the thought leadership of any organization rests.

---

[34]J. Boardman and B. Sauser. 2013. *Systemic Thinking: Building Maps for Worlds of Systems* (Hoboken, NJ: Wiley).

[35]C. Acklin, L. Cruickshank and M. Evans. 2013. Challenges of introducing new design and design management knowledge into the innovation activities of SMEs with little or no prior design experience. *Proceedings from 10th European Academy of Design Conference – 'Crafting the Future'*, April 17–19, 2013. Gothenburg.

Crucial Difference # 3

Design Management requires process coordination and optimization skills, whereas design thinking requires visionary leadership.

A third distinction between design thinking and design management can be found when taking a closer look at which competences and skills are needed to take the lead and responsibility for each one of the concepts. Considerable literature already exists on the variety of skills needed to design and manage design processes – for design practice and design management respectively. An example can be found in the standard textbook about design management by one of the authors of this book, referring to studies showing that the design management career path, in general, can be divided into five phases. Each one of these phases requires different skills and competences, often starting with design and development skills, followed by coordination skills, team management skills and general management skills, ultimately arriving at the skills needed to undertake strategic leadership.[36] Often, but by no means always, design managers are originally trained as designers to gradually find the strategic dimensions of design management either as interesting as or more alluring than design making, thus using their professional design practice as a stepping stone to design management – and for some further on to design leadership. In the book *Design Project Management*, the prerequisites for success as a design manager are captured in two sentences:

> *The successful design manager is likely to have experience of and/or qualifications in a creative/design background and is likely to combine this with pragmatic sensibilities and experience of and/or qualifications in business studies. Presentation and communication skills and information management skills are other essentials.*[37]

Less unambiguous are the thoughts, reflections, and observations on which skills are prerequisites for design thinking. Much of what has been

---

[36]B. Borja de Mozota. 2003. *Design Management: Using Design to Build Brand Value and Corporate Innovation* (Sacramento, CA: DMI/Allworth).

[37]G. Boyle. 2003. *Design Project Management* (London, UK: Ashgate).

written about design thinking as a concept refers to it as a way of working and thinking, which is inspired by the skills and processes ascribed to design professionals. Some of the more tangible reflections as such are those of Tim Brown and Roger Martin, as combined in the latter's book about the design of business:

> *Design thinking is a discipline that uses the designer's sensibility and methods to match people's needs with what is technologically feasible and what a viable business strategy can convert into customer value and market opportunity.*[38]

To this Roger Martin adds that

> *A person or organization instilled with that discipline is constantly seeking a fruitful balance between reliability and validity, between art and science, between intuition and analytics, and between exploration and exploitation. The design-thinking organization applies the designer's most crucial tool to the problems of business. That tool is* 'abductive reasoning'.[39]

Martin explains his point of view by juxtaposing the term with "deductive reasoning" – based on the logic of what must be, from the general to the specific – and with "inductive reasoning" – based on the logic of what is operative, from the specific to the general. "Abductive reasoning," he explains, was introduced by philosopher Charles Sanders Peirce, and is based not on observations of what exists but on wondering what could be. That is the hallmark of the designer, and also of those adopting design thinking, namely, being able to work systematically with what could be – with what others call visions and long-term strategic goals – and shaping the culture needed to undertake that journey. In other words, what we otherwise associate with true leadership. The deductive reasoning, provided the three foregoing assumptions are valid, is that

[38]T. Brown. June 2008. *Design Thinking* (Boston, MA: Harvard Business Review).

[39]R. Martin. 2009. *The Design of Business: Why Design Thinking is the Next Competitive Advantage* (Boston, MA: Harvard Business Press).

> ***[t]he core of design thinking is to inspire a better vision and better leadership, whereas the core of design management is to enable organizations and their design managers to deliver on the visions gouged out by their leaders.***

What, then, is new compared with all the existing literature on design management and design thinking? First and foremost, most of what already exists, both of scholarly and of more popular literature, focuses on either design thinking **or** design management, whereas only a few papers attempt to sort out their internal correlations. One article that has been of particular importance in differentiating between the two concepts was published in the *DMI Review* in 2009. It describes both the progression of design management and the changing role of design thinking in detail. As for the sought-after distinction, the article sums it up thus:

> *In regions, where design management has a tradition, academic research begins to inform these practices, complemented by professional reflections. However, the design thinking underlying these design management practices and research tends to remain product-centric. In turn, this begins to change in regions where design has been established as part of an organization. Here, we can see how design thinking is freeing itself from these previous traditions and emerging as a practice independent from the product. Instead, design thinking now focuses on the characteristics of a problem that needs solving.*[40]

This view coincides nicely with the third quadrant of the "Four Powers of Design" model, which was previously discussed, the power called *"Design as vision. Beyond 'Advanced Design',"* including the following elements*: Strategic value, Vision, Prospective, Change management, Empowerment, Knowledge learning process, and Imagination.*[41] An interesting key word here is "empowerment," which could easily translate as "giving the mandate to," differing slightly from its related "enablement" – on a more

---

[40]R. Cooper, S. Junginger and T. Lockwood. October 2009. "Design Thinking and Design Management: A Research and Practice Perspective," *DMI Review* 20, no. 2.

[41]B. Borja de Mozota. 2002 – reprint in 2006. "The Four Powers of Design – A Value Model in Design Management," *Design Management Review* 17, no. 2.

practical note suggesting the supply of the means, knowledge, or opportunity, making feasible or possible, and providing the capacity to do something. Design thinking empowers, informs, creates an atmosphere for, inspires, and makes it meaningful to allocate resources to problem finding, scoping, framing, and reframing; to engage users, work with visualizations and prototyping; and to benefit from the value that design adds to products, services, environments, processes, communication, systems, and structures. Yet, as emphasized earlier, our mission is just as much to identify kinship between the three levels. The ten principles of good design enunciated by one of the most iconic masters of European industrial design, Dieter Rams, seem to be as true and valid today as when they were formulated almost 50 years ago. Good design is

- *innovative*
- *useful*
- *aesthetic*
- *understandable*
- *unobtrusive*
- *honest*
- *long lasting*
- *consistent down to the last detail*
- *environmentally friendly*
- *as little design as possible*

These are not descriptive of one specific solution. They are transversal values, guiding principles on the basis of which any decision could be made. If "good design" were exchanged with "good design management," or even "good design leadership," they would be equally valid.

Crucial Difference # 4

Design Thinking provides the vision and leadership (empowers); design management the business case (enables).

This hierarchical approach to distinguishing the two is clearly reflected earlier in this book and hence must serve as a reminder. Our firm belief is that the two reflect most other components of organizational life; the premises and direction are defined on a higher level than where the means to pursue the vision is embedded. One could claim, for the sake of argument, that without a clear mandate from the top the resources to apply design management professionally rarely exist. Design thinking empowers through its relevance to defining an organization's DNA:

> *Design thinking addresses the fundamental assumptions, values, norms, and beliefs that make an organization what it is.*

Design management, on the other hand, can be applied as a business case format throughout an organization, provided the value of design resonates at the very top of the hierarchy:

> *We would like to argue that the rise in design thinking has helped to raise awareness of design management at different levels in the organization and, with that, has contributed to a clearer picture of design management.*[42]

And unless we disentangle the two, we are not only adding to the confusion and passing up the synergies between them, but also risking the loss of the inherent potential of either one.

---

[42]R. Cooper, S. Junginger and T. Lockwood. October 2009. "Design Thinking and Design Management: A Research and Practice Perspective," *DMI Review*, 20, no. 2.

PART 6

Design thinking – as opposed to design and design management – is not a function but a doctrine, and, as such, no less than a credendum that the entire organization and all its parts need to abide by.

From Design Excellence to Design as Core Competency

In all walks of life, bringing ideas to life can be a barrier. Good intentions often stay exactly that – intentions – and many great ideas never leave the minds of their originators or the organizations or teams in which they were incubated. This lack of executional power or implementation abilities is potentially fatal if it occurs in fast-moving environments, where not only thinking about change, but also actually bringing ideas to market is crucial for survival.

> *Increasingly, organizational analysts identify failure of implementation, innovation failure as the cause of many organizations' inability to achieve the intended benefits of the innovations they adopt.*[1]

Researchers Klein and Sorra identified the determining factors of an organization's success rate in implementing innovation and change to be a climate characterized by the right skills, the right incentives and disincentives, and the absence of obstacles for implementation – in combination

[1]K.J. Klein and J.S. Sorra. October 1996. "The Challenge of Innovation Implementation," *The Academy of Management Review* 21, no. 4, pp. 1055-1080.

with a commitment from the guardians of the organizational values. In other words, appropriate management skills need to coexist with leadership commitment to guarantee successful implementation. Likewise, to truly benefit from design, the *design* itself, the *management* of design, design *thinking*, and *leadership commitment* are all needed (Figure 11). Hence, our reasoning and model entail that

Design excellence = ***great design*** + ***design management*** + ***design thinking*** + ***leadership***

Figure 11 Borja de Mozota and Valade-Amland: The Design Excellence Loop

Although design, design management, and design thinking have all been subject to extensive research and scholarly attention, design excellence serves primarily as a "label" used to award solutions, deemed to be excellent within their own categories of products or services and assessed according to some predefined criteria. We find the term "design excellence" interesting and appropriate to describe situations where design thinking exists as a premise and where design management has been applied professionally and successfully and adapted to the challenge or process in question.

Regardless of sector, industry, or organizational set-up, an increasing number of real-life experiences and studies point in the direction of an inescapable connectedness between design, design management, and design thinking, as well as a clear cause–effect relation or consequence entailing the extent to which and how design is embraced by an organization. Our assumption is that design – having been around since the beginning of human civilization – at one point in time, as design became recognized as a professional, structured, and replicable activity, fostered the need for a specific variety of project management, a discipline that already existed for ages but started taking shape from the late 1950s onward.[2] This point in time emerged in the late seventies, and design management found its

---

[2]T. Seymour and S. Hussein. 2014. "The History of Project Management," *International Journal of Management & Information Systems* 18, no. 4.

form in the eighties, where it gradually captured its own space and identity in the design and design research communities, as well as in education. It started as a clearly defined approach to managing design projects but slowly came to encompass the art of building a "design culture" within an organization. Where this dimension of design management proved successful, the somewhat more strategic and often C-level engagement in design at one point had become so massive in terms of interest both from academia and the boardrooms around the world that it was considered worthy of being "rebranded" as design thinking. And where design thinking reigns, the use of design and the development of the mechanisms needed to manage and benefit fully from design are regarded as just instrumental building blocks of corporate or organizational strategies, as are finances, human resources, investor relations, and public affairs.

Design has traditionally and most often embodied products and services, whereas design management plays a distinct role in enabling design and designers to do so, in the form of brand guardianship and strategic gatekeeping. Design thinking provides for inspiration and for the mandate and support needed for the organization to fully exploit design's potential (Figure 12).

Figure 12 Borja de Mozota and Valade-Amland: The Products, Brand and Organization Loop

To make sure that we do not add to the confusion, but rather cast some light over the field, we would like to contextualize our terminology in a manner that underpins our claim: ***design***, ***design management***, ***design thinking*** (or design leadership), and ***design excellence***. We will do this by latching the four concepts onto the Montréal Design Declaration, endorsed by more than a dozen international bodies, including the United Nations Educational, Scientific and Cultural Organization (UNESCO), because it is the closest we've ever come to universal consensus around the meaning, role, and value of design. It suddenly becomes evident that, as a whole, the eight aspirations of the global design community on behalf of its core interest, design, can be achieved only if it exists in all four forms. It even requires that design at large is embraced and appreciated by world leaders, international organizations, and policy makers, which has, incidentally, proven to be an easier battle than to convince many business leaders:

The Montreal Design Declaration defines the Value of Design through eight bold propositions:

- *Design is a driver of innovation and competition, growth and development, efficiency and prosperity.*
- *Design is an agent for sustainable solutions.*
- *Design expresses culture.*
- *Design adds value to technology.*
- *Design facilitates change.*
- *Design introduces intelligence to cities.*
- *Design addresses resiliency and manages risk.*
- *Design fosters development.*[3]

Strategic Intent and Design Governance

Delivering on these overriding and somehow all-encompassing ambitions, shared by most organizations around the world, requires, first of all, the existence of a clear and unambiguous intent, which is indisputably a leadership responsibility: design leadership, if you wish. This, fundamentally spoken, materializes in an informed mandate from the very top of the organization to pursue development goals by applying and integrating design methodologies, design processes, design principles, and design management in all relevant strategies and operations. This is how design thinking inspires and empowers. Assuming that such an intent exists and is known to all, as well as adopted throughout the organization, the exploration and assessment of new technologies and materials becomes a design management priority. The same applies to making sure that their application supports not only the organization's own intent and delivery, on and beyond the expectations of the user, but also the aspirations

[3]*Montréal Design Declaration* – Press release issued on November 9, 2017 at the first World Design Summit in Montréal.

of the organization vis-à-vis its concerns in the pursuit of meeting the sustainable development goals.[4] Exploiting technological developments and turning data into valuable market intelligence to the benefit of one's own competitive advantage, yet still reducing one's footprint and complying with or aiming at transcending best practices with regard to governance and responsibility, requires true design leadership throughout the organization as well as professionalism and decision-making capacity on strategic, tactical, and operational levels. The role of design leadership and design management in a context of innovation was quite effectively spelled out in an article in 2005, albeit without using the term design thinking:

> *Creating an environment in which challenging the status quo is actively encouraged is at the heart of the innovation process. This process needs clear, firm leadership, and it's the design leader's responsibility to do just that – to make innovation part of the business' DNA. It is then the job of the design manager to help realize the innovative thinking.*[5]

Design's significance as both a driver and a catalyst of innovation has increasingly been recognized by the world community:

> *The OECD/NESTI project has identified, through available and experimental measures and analysis, considerable evidence for the integrative role of design and designers between creative development efforts, the practice of innovation in firms, and the implementation of innovations in the marketplace. It is not only an activity carried out by specialized personnel in specific settings but is also a process that can systematically influence most of the activities usually contributing to business innovation projects.*[6]

---

[4]United Nations. 2015. *Transforming Our World: the 2030 Agenda for Sustainable Development*, Resolution 70/1 adopted by the General Assembly on September 25, 2015.

[5]R. Turner, Y. Weisbarth, K. Ekuan, G. Zaccai, P. Picaud, and P. Haythornthwaite. Spring 2005. "Insights on Innovation," *Design Management Review* 16, no. 2, pp. 16-22.

[6]F. Galindo-Rueda and V. Millot. 2015. *Measuring Design and its Role in Innovation*, OECD Science, Technology and Industry Working Papers, 2015/01, OECD Publishing.

One reason for the role of design as a tool of innovation being more widely accepted might be its historical connotation of linking design to the invention and development of new physical products – thus also the key pillar in the innovation discourse, for centuries. However, studies show that design is exactly as valuable for companies whose core activity is intangible services – as opposed to tangible products – as for companies whose products and services are of equal importance.[7] In line with our discussion about design and the overall intent, sustainable solutions require endorsement from the very top of the organization as much as they require knowledge about materials and processes and value chains in the parts of the organization dedicated to continuous improvement and innovation. Very few chief executive officers have the time and background needed to stay on top of new polymers or composites, sintering techniques or 3D printing processes, additive technologies or intelligent materials. This is not only because these are all demanding areas of science and expertise, but because the speed at which such new technologies are developed and improved is mind-blowing. In addition, of course, managing a medium or large company implies equally demanding expertise within other areas of business development and management. Having said that, also very few designers are able to keep track of these developments, but a pivotal part of design practice is to research and test, experiment with, and consider potentially relevant and useful new materials and technologies to enhance existing or develop new competitive products or solutions, including the considerations need to minimize their footprint throughout the entire life cycle, and including empathy for user needs and preferences. This requires not only an interest among design practitioners and endorsement from the top, but also a clear strategy for how design is used from operation to operation or department to department; in other words, design management.

In his book *In the Bubble*, the esteemed, although not entirely uncontroversial, design thinker John Thackara lists what he refers to as "design

---

[7]M. Candi. 2005. *Design as an Element of Innovation: Evaluating Design Emphasis and Focus in New Technology Firms* (Reykjavik, Iceland: School of Business, University of Reykjavik).

mindfulness," driven by sensitivity to context, to relationships, and to consequences[8]:

- *Think about the consequences of design actions and pay close attention to the natural, industrial and cultural systems that are the context of design actions*
- *Consider material and energy flows in all designed systems*
- *Give priority to human agency and not treat humans as a 'factor' in some bigger picture*
- *Deliver value to people – not deliver people to systems*
- *Treat 'content' as something we do, not something we are sold*
- *Treat place, time and cultural difference as positive values, not as obstacles*
- *Focus on services, not on things, and refrain from flooding the world with pointless devices*

Not only do most designers already demonstrate the sensitivity Thackara calls for, but some of the world's most successful companies are guided by similar principles.

> *In what it creates, for whom it creates, in where and how it creates, and in relationships with consumers and communities, an organization's design team can help lead Corporate Social Responsibility.*[9]

As the design profession has become more and more recognized as research and knowledge based, a paradigm shift has taken place, from being project oriented to being predominantly process oriented. Designers are more than just problem solvers; they are also drivers of the dynamics of knowledge building in organizations through research:

> *The activity of design consists in the transformation of an input representation into an output representation. In an activity that functions*

---

[8]J. Thackara. 2005. *In the Bubble: Designing in a Complex World* (Cambridge, MA: MIT Press).

[9]Y. Koo and R. Cooper. 2011. "Managing Corporate Social Responsibility through Design," *DMI Review* 22, no. 1.

by way of representations, knowledge plays a central role. Designing is a cognitive activity.[10]

Moreover,

Prahalad and Hamel argue that information-based invisible assets such as technology, customer trust, brand image, corporate culture and management skills are the real resources of competitive advantage, because they are difficult and time consuming to accumulate, and can be used in multiple ways simultaneously. To design managers, it means assessing design value as a resource that is rare, inimitable, and non-substitutable; it also means managing design with the long-term perspective of sustained competitive advantage rather than a short-term view of project management.[11]

This new evidence of design as a resource and core competency comes from another theory of strategy, known as the Resource Based View (RBV). Could this theory explain the value of design thinking as the value of a set of specific key skills embedded in design thinking? The RBV of strategy claims that the development of valuable, rare, difficult to imitate, and nonsubstitutable resources results in sustained superior performance. It emphasizes the ability to recognize the importance of invisible assets to build competitive advantage as a core competency. It gives value to the way you embed design in the organization or what is also called a "design you can't see" strategy (Figure 13).

The design industry is part of the creative industries, whose value has been studied and included in national statistics of economic performance all over the world for decades. Recently, studies from various sources have focused more specifically on the business value of design. The *McKinsey Quarterly* (October 2018) report insists on the value of measuring and driving design performance, stating that *Design is more than a feeling; it is a CEO-level priority for growth and long-term performance.* Behind this

---

[10]W. Visser. 2006. *The Cognitive Artifacts of Designing* (New York, NY: Routledge).

[11]B. Borja de Mozota. 2011. *Handbook of Design Management Research,* Chapter 18: Design Strategic Value Revisited, pp. 278-93.

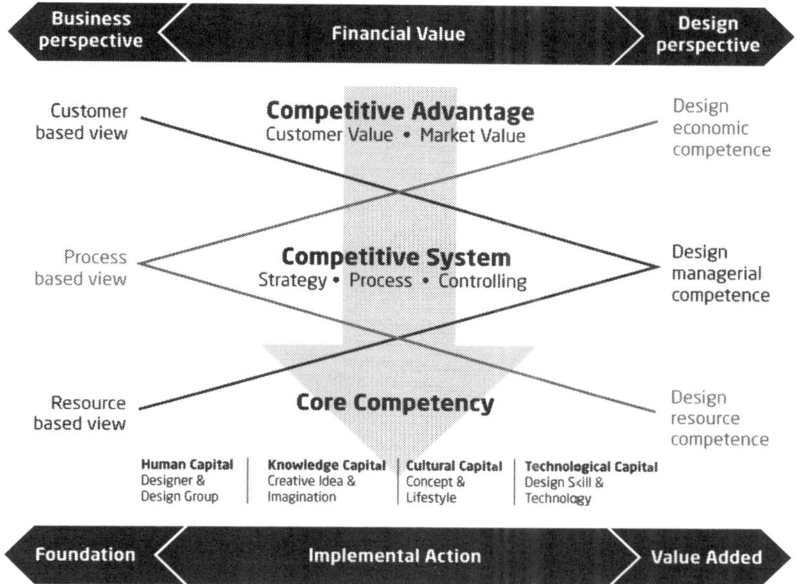

***Figure 13** Borja de Mozota and Kim. 2009. From Design Excellence to Design as Core Competence*

trend toward widespread acknowledgment of design indicators, there is an emerging understanding that the value of design can be measured on numerous levels beyond seeing design as "competitive advantage" that is immediately visible in the market – what has for many years been labeled design as differentiator.

> *In summary, when pleading for strategic design, design managers, designers and design educators should explain what their definition of strategy is, whether they refer to strategy as an external competitive advantage or strategy as a resource and internal sustained advantage. Additionally, if they want to adopt a prospective and contemporary view of design strategy, they may turn their vision far from designing artefacts to rather designing the organization resources and its knowledge capital.*[12]

[12]B. Borja de Mozota and B. Y. Kim. 2009. "From Design as Fit to Design as Resource," *DMI Review* 20/2, pp. 66–76.

The buzz of design thinking is the buzz of adopting empathy in user-centered organizations and the recognition of the empathic skills of designers as fundamental to helping the entire organization run their activities closer to the needs of the market and their consumers. And it is true that innovation success and performance in many organizations are based on the ability to build a consumer-centric culture. As a matter of fact, the current digital transformation entails cultural transformation, which in turn demands designer skills, whether focusing on managers learning to think more like designers or on giving design functions the autonomy to drive the cultural change.

As a matter of fact, the business value of design is surprisingly well documented. In a European study from 2002, the CEOs of 33 companies, all of which had received design awards in their own countries, were asked to classify 21 variables of where design creates value (Figure 14):

6 = fundamental, 5 = very important, 4 = important	Mean	Dispersion
Design creates a competitive advantage	5.39	0.55
Design is a core competency	5.12	1.04
Design contributes significantly to benefits perceived by consumers	5.00	0.97
Design changes the spirit of the firm that becomes more innovative	4.94	0.86
Design develops exports	4.88	1.15
Design increases market share	4.75	0.94
Design allows the company to sell at a higher price	4.69	1.16
Design improves co-ordination between marketing and R&D functions	4.68	1.07
Design is a know-how that transforms the activity processes	4.64	1.12
Design develops customer care in the innovation policy	4.60	1.25
Design generates technology transfers	4.22	1.47
Design gives access to a wide variety of markets	4.19	1.55
Design accelerates the launch of new products	4.07	1.28
Design improves co-ordination between production and marketing	4.00	1.16
Design develops project management of innovation	3.93	1.20
Design creates a new market	3.90	1.72
Design improves the circulation of information in innovation	3.80	1.34
Design means higher margins or costs reduction	3.80	1.31
Design is difficult to imitate by competitors	3.76	1.43
Design changes relationships with suppliers	3.70	1.23
Design improves co-operation between agents	3.64	1.18

Figure 14 Borja de Mozota. 2002. Design and Competitive Edge
Source: Borja de Mozota. 2002. Design and Competitive Edge, Academic Review - Design Management Journal 2 reprint 2011 Handbook Design Management, Research Berg.

A more recent report shows similar results, confirming that design

- ***increases speed to market***
- ***extends market reach***
- ***drives engagement and loyalty***
- ***enhances internal capabilities***
- ***inspires visionary transformation*** [13]

When discussing the strategic positioning of design in a company, the choice between design as a competitive advantage – which is "design you can see" and "design strategy as fit" – which is design as a sustained competitive advantage, has to be made. Although the first kind is prone to be copied, design as a core competency is difficult to imitate by your competitors. During strategic audits and SWOT analyses, organizations use models for assessing their external environment, such as Porter's Five Forces or PESTEL, and for carrying out internal audits, a Boston Consulting Group (BCG) matrix, a value chain model, or a Business Model Canvas. The RBV of strategy brings another model, Value, Rarity, Imitability, Organization (VRIO) to the table, building on Barney's difficult definition of core competency and sustained competitive advantage:

A resource that is valuable, rare, difficult to imitate and nonsubstitutable. [14]

The question is how to recognize and organize the management of design so as to ensure that it is rare and difficult to imitate, hence improving the organization's knowledge capital (Figure 15).

Building Design Capacity

Capacity Building in Organizations

One key player in building evidence of service design impact on the governance of organizations is Christian Bason, who, in one of his latest

[13]FROG. 2017. *The Business Value of Design* (San Francisco, CA: FROG Insights).

[14]J. Barney. 1991. "Firm Resources and Sustained Competitive Advantage," *Journal of Management* 17, no. 1, pp. 99-120.

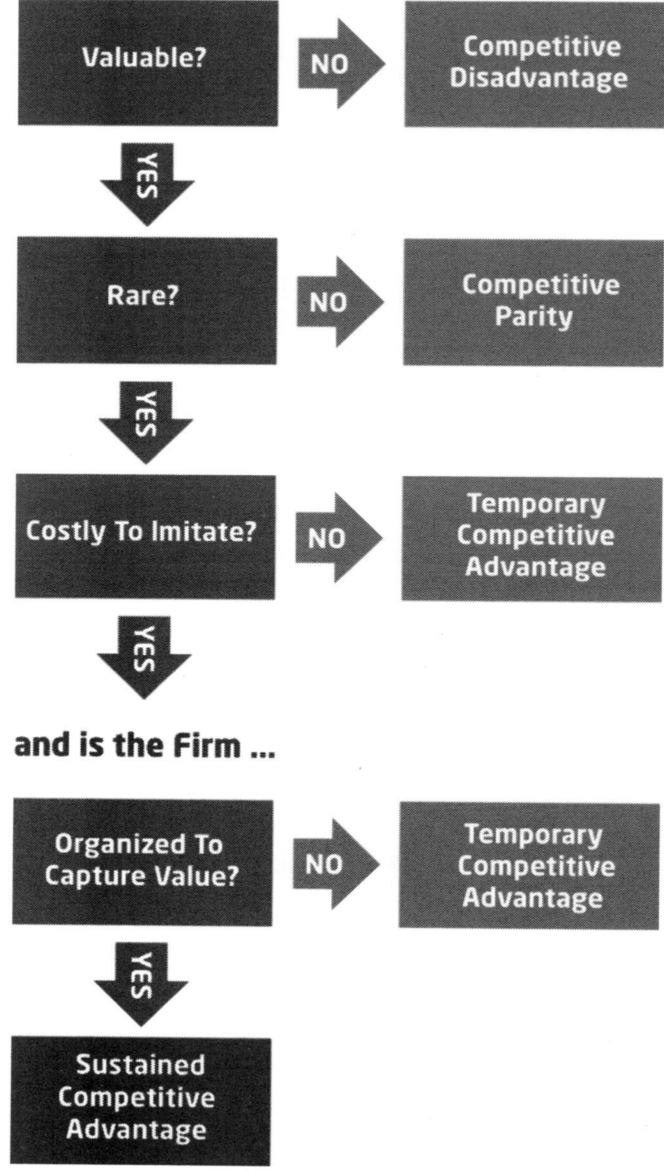

Figure 15 THE VRIO model - Barney RBV strategy.

books, set out to explore, among others, how working with design affected public sector managers:

> *Managers who use design approaches seem inclined toward governance that, in comparison to historical public management approaches are more:*
>
> - *Relational, in terms of a distinctly human and often longer-term perspective on the role of the public organization and its impact on the outside world; often this implies a reframing of the kind of value the organization is supposed to bring to citizens and society*
> - *Networked, understood as a model of governance that actively considers and includes a broad variety of societal actors to achieve public outcomes*
> - *Interactive, exhibiting increased awareness and more explicit use of (physical and virtual) artefacts in mediating purposeful interactions between the organization and citizens and other users and stakeholders; and finally, managers who use design approaches are more*
> - *Reflective, which is to say driven by a more qualitative, emphatic, subjective, and complex understanding of the organization's ability to enact change.*[15]

So in order to develop a business context that is favorable for design excellence, organizations have to consider designers' skills as more significant than the value of designers' tangible output (Figure 16).

Moreover, capacity needs to be built to ensure cultural sensitivity and differentiation. Globalization is a fact, and, to some extent, certain elements contributing to the variety and diversity one would expect when crossing borders or landing in some remote destination are slowly being eradicated. And yet regardless of how "global" we all tend to see ourselves, we respond inherently in different ways when faced with the reality of a culture to which we are not native. Hence, acknowledging and acting on

---

[15]C. Bason. 2017. *Leading Public Design: How Managers Engage with Design to Transform Public Governance* (Copenhagen: Copenhagen Business School).

Knowledge	Attitude Values	Applied skills	Understanding skills
Design process	*Risk-taking* *Managing uncertainty*	Practical design skills *Prototyping* Drawing ability	*Observation*
Material	Originality	Creative techniques Lateral thinking	Researching
Market	Anticipating future trends Forward thinking	Commercial skills	Logical thinking *Integrative thinking*
Technology	Proactive in developing relationships	Communication skills (Presentation and report writing)	Analyzing Prioritizing Structuring problems
User awareness	Open-minded	Computer skills	*Scenario building* *Narrative*
Culture	Understanding multidisciplinary context	Design for manufacture	Synthesizing *Holistic thinking*
Aesthetic awareness	*Focusing on usability*	Project management	Intuitive thinking & action
Human factors	Attention to detail	Optimization	Consumer and stakeholder needs
Manufacturing process	*Learning from errors*	*Team work*	*Human empathy*

***Figure 16* Borja de Mozota. May 2011. Designers skills in organizations; The Value of Designers' Skills in the 21st Century**

Source: Borja de Mozota. May 2011. Designers skills in organizations; The Value of Designers' Skills in the 21st Century, Design Research Society, Paris Symposium on Education.

these intrinsic, culturally rooted differences need to be, and are increasingly, reflected in design practice.

> *There is an emerging interest in the impact of cultural dimensions on the experience and interaction between people and products. Globalization has led to a situation in which product design teams from one culture or context often have to develop a product, which will be used in a (totally) other cultural environment. Globalization also confronts companies to decide between 'global' or 'local' featured design of products. As a result, it has become essential for the industrial design education and profession to take the context and culture of the end-users more serious[ly] and to look for consequences regarding industrial design.*[16]

[16] J.C. Diehl and H.H.C.M. Christiaans. Globalization and cross-cultural product design. *Proceedings from International Design Conference – Design,* May 15-18, 2006; Dubrovnik, Croatia.

Capacity Building in Strategic Design as Sensemaking

This brings us back to the concept of strategic design as sensemaking, not only as Karl Weick used the term, making sense of our surroundings, of complexity and of the changes taking place around us – or Christian Madsbjerg's large-scale making sense of a situation or a culture or a world.[17] Design is also a pivotal component in making sense of products that we rely on every day, of information overload in most human-made environments, and of instructions and day-to-day digital and real-life interaction. John Maeda's ten laws of simplicity in many ways represent a key to why design plays such an important role in building bridges between human beings and technology [18]:

1. ***Reduce:*** *The simplest way to achieve simplicity is through thoughtful reduction.*
2. ***Organize:*** *Organization makes a system of many appear fewer.*
3. ***Time:*** *Savings in time feel like simplicity.*
4. ***Learn:*** *Knowledge makes everything simpler.*
5. ***Differences:*** *Simplicity and complexity need each other.*
6. ***Context:*** *What lies in the periphery of simplicity is definitely not peripheral.*
7. ***Emotion:*** *More emotions are better than less.*
8. ***Trust:*** *In simplicity we trust.*
9. ***Failure:*** *Some things can never be made simple.*
10. ***The one:*** *Simplicity is about subtracting the obvious and adding the meaningful.*

By intuitively striving for simplicity where it is appropriate and possible, designers contribute to bridging technology with human needs, thus adding value to technology and, in turn, making technology sensible and more accessible to people, who would otherwise be prohibited from enjoying these advantages.

---

[17] C. Madsbjerg. 2017. *Sensemaking; What Makes Human Intelligence Essential in the Age of the Algorithm* (New York, NY: Little Brown Book Group).

[18] J. Maeda. 2006. *The Laws of Simplicity* (Boston, MA: MIT Press).

Capacity Building for Behavioral Change

Change is, as already discussed, not always perceived as good. However, change is a given, because the alternative is stagnation and regress. Regardless of design's role as a change agent, design alone is rarely the only factor responsible for change. But it plays a vital role in making change easier and less frightening. Moreover, we know that change rarely comes by itself; it has to be started by something or someone, as observed by the authors of the bestseller *Switch*:

> *Ultimately, all change efforts boil down to the same mission: Can you get people to start behaving in a new way?*[19]

Designers are rarely the ones who start behaving differently, but more often than we think the works of designers enable people to do so. Such changes can be prompted by user-friendly products, technologies, and digital applications, enabling concepts such as the sharing economy to flourish and home-based work to be a real alternative to spending time on commuting to an office, where exactly the same amount and quality of work would be delivered. Change can also be designed through subtle incentives to do something different or differently, also often referred to as ***choice architecture*** or ***nudging***.[20] Finally, people's behavior is hugely influenced by communication design – from visual effects and ads to wayfinding and information design, by the design of physical environments, urban design, and affordances, and by service design, guiding our behavior vis-à-vis the providers of private or public sector services. This knowledge has been systematically exploited as a competitive tool for decades – even centuries – but has also increasingly been discovered by the public sectors of this world, not necessarily as a competitive tool as such, but as a proven, effective means to provide better or smarter services at a lower cost.

---

[19]C. Heath and D. Heath. 2010. *Switch: How to Change Things When Change is Hard* (New York, NY: Thorndike Press).

[20]R.H. Thaler and C.R. Sunstein. 2008. *Nudge – Improving Decisions about Health, Wealth and Happiness* (London, UK: Penguin).

One of the areas where service design, in particular, has resonated surprisingly fast and well is within the public health and care sectors. For a long time, service design was almost synonymous with public sector design, until the private sector decided to be more overt about their use of and dependence on design. One of the pioneering suppliers of service design, LiveWork, calls it "humanising of services."

> *In order to innovate the system of public services there is a need to step outside the box, get deep insights into the system from different perspectives, to radically reframe the problem, expand the system, ideate with relevant stakeholders and to develop prototypes that can be tested and refined: there is a proven need for service design. And these new ways of approaching challenges using the processes and methods of service design have to be brought inside the organisation, so training and capacity building are crucial to enable public sector organisations to re-invent themselves and their relationship to their citizens.*[21]

Although the public sectors in some countries have thrown themselves wholeheartedly into service design and user-centered innovation, until now the endeavors have been fairly explorative, because hard evidence of design's appropriateness vis-à-vis the challenges faced by the public sector has been scarce. Moreover, the enthusiasm for design has not always enjoyed the company of design management expertise, sometimes reducing the measurable effects of the sector's endeavors.

Hence, much speaks to the advantage of design as a more holistic approach to the development of public services than other, more traditional approaches, emphasizing the experienced and long-term qualitative value rather than a shorter-term, single bottom line cost-benefit equation. We will revert to the specific area of service design later – for one very good reason…

---

[21] Service Design Network/Netherlands Enterprise Agency. 2016. *Service Design Impact Report: Public Sector*, Cologne, Germany.

Design Ability for Systemic Thinking

Another factor that adds to the rationale is the degree of complexity and need for systemic thinking.

> *The more we study the major problems of our time, the more we come to realise that they cannot be understood in isolation. They are systemic problems, which means that they are interconnected and interdependent.*[22]

One can design an individual artefact in its own right, without depending on or assessing its connectedness to other products or contexts, even though a fundamental understanding of the context in which and by whom the object will be used will in most cases enhance the overall assessment of the design object. Services are intrinsically more dependent on the context in which they will be experienced, and organizational design has a clear systemic element per se. Design management also exists in an environment of determining factors and is thus somewhat influenced by and clearly benefits from systemic thinking, whereas design thinking is essentially systemic by nature. Whether or not a situation will benefit from systemic thinking can be tested quite simply by asking **(1)** ***whether it consists of a whole that is made up of any number of identifiable elements***, **(2)** ***whether these elements are interconnected such that intervening with one element also affects one or several of the other elements and/or on the whole***, and **(3)** ***whether there are multiple, nonlinear connections and feedback systems between the elements***. Applying systems thinking starts with

1. ***recognizing interconnectedness,***
2. ***identifying and understanding feedback***
3. ***understanding system structure***
4. ***differentiating types of stocks, flows, and variables***
5. ***identifying and understanding nonlinear relationships***

---

[22]F. Capra. 1996. *The Web of Life: A New Synthesis of Mind and Matter* (London, UK: Flamingo).

6. ***understanding dynamic behavior***
7. ***reducing complexity by modeling systems conceptually, and***
8. ***understanding systems at different scales.***

The effect of applying systems thinking is improvement of the capability to identify and understand systems, predicting their behaviors, and devising modifications to them in order to produce desired effects.[23] As such, there is an obvious kinship between systemic problems and wicked problems, which we discussed briefly at the very beginning of this book.

> *Design is increasingly involved in the discourse around so-called "wicked" problems – either because we are complicit in their creation or drawn to the complexity of design opportunity that surrounds them. These are the Lernaean Hydrae of design challenges – for every tangible facet of the problem we address an increasingly complex web of both tangible and intangible problems grows in its place. The potential contexts of design action within these wicked problems are dynamic, characterized by complex interdependencies, and difficult to identify.*

This bridge is supported by four basic assertions about the intrinsic relation of contemporary design practice to systems thinking;

> *Assertion #1: One cannot design sustainably outside the space of systems.*
> *Assertion #2: One cannot design empathically outside the space of systems.*
> *Assertion #3: One cannot innovate outside the space of systems.*
> *Assertion #4: One cannot teach design for this century outside of the space of systems* [24]

Don Norman, hence, was only partially right in his assumption that we are faced with a fork in the road, with two different possible futures for design: (1) A craft and practice; (2) A mode of thinking. Although it is true

---

[23]R.D. Arnold. 2015. *A Definition of Systems Thinking: A Systems Approach,* 2015 Conference on Systems Engineering Research.

[24]P. Beirne. 2014. *Wicked Design 101: Teaching to the complexity of our times,* Relating Systems Thinking and Design 2014 working paper.

that a substantial part of the design stories that we encounter today seem to deal with either the one or the other, we also see design following a third future, embracing both design as a craft and practice and design as a mode of thinking – and what bridges the two is design management. This future is where design creates the utmost value. The need for design management to truly benefit from design as a representation, designed objects and services, has already been demonstrated,[25] whereas it is still an assumption on our part that design excellence is achieved only where the entire palette of design effectiveness is brought into play to empower, enable, and embody.

The Primacy of Purpose

The purpose of a system is the reason ***why*** it exists. The only hope of getting people with all kinds of backgrounds and life projects to work together is a strong, organizing purpose, in a healthy organization. Goals support the mission and vision, whereas the mission and vision support the purpose. Julie Zhuo, former manager of Facebook's design team, insists that purpose, people, and process are the three things managers think about all day. The why, the who, the how: three early phases of any creative design process.

> *Good design at its core is about understanding people and their needs in order to create the best possible tools for them. I am drawn to design for a lot of the same reasons that I am drawn to management – it feels like a deeply human endeavor to empower others.*[26]

Designers' Skills and Role

Designers' Skills as Driver of Management Value

It would be odd if others were better at delivering design as we traditionally know it than people who trained to become professional design practitioners; the embodiment of strategies into products and services with

---

[25]A. Fernández-Mesa, J. Alegre-Vidal, R. Chiva-Gómez and A. Gutiérrez-Gracia. 2012. *Design Management Capability: Its Mediating Role between Organizational Learning Capability and Innovation Performance in SMEs.*

[26]J. Zhuo. 2019. *The Making of a Manager* (New York, NY: Portfolio/Penguin).

due concern for the needs of people, organizations and the future – for people, profit, and planet, vested in their deep understanding of materials and functionality, of user experience, and of beauty. Even though amateurs and even professionals of inferior quality will always occupy a certain space in all markets, the acknowledgment of professional designers and their contribution to both our quality of life and to our economies seems to be rather firmly rooted.

> *Design as a highly complex and sophisticated skill. It is not a mystical ability given only to those with recondite powers, but a skill, which, for many, must be learnt and practiced rather like the playing of a sport or a musical instrument.*[27]

So how are designers' skills important for business? In his recent work, Kamil Michelswki classified five distinctive aspects of design as a professional culture:

> ***Embracing uncertainty and ambiguity:*** *Designers know that when it comes to creating something completely new and original, they are no guarantee of success. They realise and accept that a really creative process is often discontinuous and messy. This allows them to change the received wisdom with conviction and fearlessness. It is not difficult to see how this attitude may be a good basis for coming up with breakthrough ideas and conviction.*
>
> ***Engaging deep empathy:*** *Using true empathy requires courage, honesty and abandoning one's mental models. Designers treat these consumers as real human beings and not simply as management abstraction.*
>
> ***Embracing the power of the five senses:*** *Designers recognize that two senses, namely sight and hearing, are often not enough to create something that captivates people on a deep, visceral level. Their attitude towards using their sense of aesthetics is honest and open. They are happy to use apparent complexity to create surprise and delight.*

[27]B. Lawson. 2005. *How Designers Think: The Design Process Demystified* (London, UK: Elsevier Architectural Press).

Playfully bringing things to life: *In order to create an innovative process and dialogue, designers believe in the power of playfulness, humour and a healthy dose of subversion. They often use the cloak of creativity and apparent silliness, projected into them by other professions, to ask some profound questions and challenge entrenched ways of doing things. Creatively manifesting potential products, services and future scenarios as quickly is effectively their way of being.*

Creating new meaning from complexity: *At the heart of designers' ways of doing things is the willingness to engage and to reconcile multiple, often contradictory, points of view and sources of information in order to come up with an entirely new way of thinking about something. Strategy is one thing but turning all the disparate elements into a coherent and delightful whole is something else entirely.* [28]

Designers' skills therefore impact organizations by spreading their values and ways of doing things.

Their connections to the professional group closest to their own, namely marketers, can potentially be detrimental to the way in which designers and design attitude are seen in organizations. The power balance is levelling out, but power still predominantly rests with the marketers, once again citing Michlewski:

Designers are the invaders of the corporate world whilst marketers are the natives at the strategic level.

Design management character requires the understanding of design processes, but also of project and process management. Furthermore, there are various levels of design management – operational, functional, and strategic – for which different skills and professional profiles are needed.[29]

---

[28]K. Michlewski. 2015. *Design Attitude* (London, UK: Gower).

[29]B. Borja de Mozota. 2003. *Design Management – Using Design to Build Brand Value and Corporate Innovation* (Sacramento, CA: DMI/Allworth).

We have seen designers with a flair for management developing into first class representatives of all forms of design management, just as we have seen equivalent design managers coming from management careers and business schools. Thus, although there is no unambiguous road toward a career as design manager, there might be another, subtler prerequisite. A design manager needs to constantly negotiate between the creative aspirations of the designer or design team, on the one hand, and the limitations laid out in the design brief, the expectations of the client organization, whether internal or external, and the changing priorities and constant competition for a space in the minds of the senior management, on the other. And one has to love every bit of it, which narrows the field of talented design managers significantly.

The agents of the more strategic approach to design management in an organization hold hands with its conveyors of design thinking, and, as previously argued, design thinking resides in a deeply rooted understanding of the value of design in all its forms and shapes. A designer or design team as well as any design manager might be overt advocates of design thinking in an organization, regardless of the degree of resonance, but for design thinking to truly add any value to an organization, it needs to be embraced by and firmly rooted in the senior management and filter down throughout the entire organism.

Thus, design thinking – as opposed to design and design management – is not a function but a doctrine, and as such no less than a credendum to which the entire organization and all its parts need to abide by.

Approaching any creative job from a strategic standpoint is much more effective than a tactical execution-based approach. Although it might take longer in terms of up-front research, it yields better results. But for this to happen, new design leaders need to agree to share with business some common concepts: ***purpose, process, sustainable change, people, insights, strategy, value,*** and ***qualitative metrics.***

Strategic Designers' Role as the Future Agents for Change

Beyond the common understanding of design contributing to human-centered organizations, Heather Fraser considers three gears for business design, claiming that *Business design is an exercise in agility: emotionally, tactically and cognitively*

- *empathy and deep human understanding*
- *concept visualization for holistic solutions that better meet the needs of your customers and other stakeholders*
- *a strategy to deliver and scale the idea process to refocus your resources in a more effective way*[30]

Along the same lines of rationale, a recent book discussing the connections between designers' skills and performance introduces the idea of seven role models for designers in organizations:

The seven roles that designers can adhere to in order to drive change in organizations are as follows:

- *Cultural catalyst*
- *Framework maker*
- *Humaniser*
- *Power broker*
- *Friendly challenger*
- *Technology enabler, Community builder*[31]

So, paradoxically, although design has become somewhat banalized, it has also moved up the value chain and become a boardroom topic, as reflected in these two observations:

---

[30]H.M.A. Fraser. 2019. *Design Works: A Guide to Creating and Sustaining Value through Business Design* (Toronto, ON, Canada: Rotman).

[31]J. Yee, E. Jefferies and K. Michlewski. 2017. *Transformations: 7 Roles to Drive Change by Design* (Amsterdam: BIS Publishers).

Design seems to have moved from being a specialized competence of professions rooted in industrialized economies, to become something we can all practice as part of our consumption activities.[32]

and

The emphasis on design clearly is moving to the C-suite, and more and more organizations are creating a chief design officer role.[33]

For the concept of design, this ambiguity has existed for more than two decades, whereas it has been increasingly visible for the concept of design thinking since it was truly revitalized through Tim Brown's book in 2009.[34] And, in the meantime, the concept of design management almost disappeared from the radar.[35] This has contributed to a distortion in both ends, as design and design thinking – hence also their organizational role as well as what it takes to excel in either of the two – have seemed to blend into a merged and consequently quite muddled picture, as well as jeopardizing their own future relevance.

Design thinking is situated in a kind of abeyance. Its further development appears to be open in all directions.[36]

Undertaking change driven by design means that design thinking and design management, as well as design skills and competences,

---

[32]L. Kimbell. 2009. *Beyond Design Thinking: Design-as-Practice and Designs-in-Practice.* Paper presented at the CRESC Conference, September 2009, Manchester, UK.
[33]A. Ignatius. September 2015. *Design as Strategy* (Boston, MA: Harvard Business Review).
[34]T. Brown. 2009. *Change by Design: How Design Thinking Transforms Organizations and Inspires Innovation* (New York, NY: Harper Collins).
[35]Pollen Trend Consulting. 2017. Twitter Conversation Analysis on Design Management Hashtags 10.2.2017-10.3.2017 showed the occurrence of "Design Thinking" 10416 times, while "Design Management" occurred 91 times during the same period.
[36]A. Papadopoulos. 2012. *Design Thinking – Factors Influencing the Current and Future Adoption of Design Thinking within Design-Thinking-Experienced Companies* [Master Thesis], Copenhagen: Copenhagen Business School.

need to be embraced. Moreover, depending on the organizational and decision-making level you choose to integrate design, different design-specific skills will be required to foster a specific type of change.

Inspire, Humanize, Experience

External forces for change are disturbing to all organizations, whether the change stems from increased globalization, digitization, demands for more sustainable solutions, gender and demographic issues, the defiance of institutions, personalization of consumption, or any other megatrend; all these external forces demand from companies that they revise their basic objectives.

Where the old world was characterized by a division between purpose-driven social organizations and profit-driven businesses, in the new world, purpose and profit go hand in hand. This also contributes to reframing the role of designers; reanimating their traditional attitude, ethics and mindsets; the design approach of applying outside-in rather than inside-out perspectives and of creating visual or tangible representations that build a set of shared references to align perceptions across functions, teams, and levels.

Social design has become increasingly attractive among designers, as governments are increasingly acknowledging design's potential to address complex problems, whether aimed at improving the conditions of marginalized groups or the performance of public sector bodies. Social design is design that exists to improve society at large, and only when behaviors are facilitated, fostered, changed, or diminished does design contribute to social change. Behaviors are instrumental to societal transformation that can be managed and measured. However, it would be irresponsible to disregard that

> *very few designers recognize that they are actually fighting the problems their disciplines helped to create and keep creating. This sounds disturbing but the designers' share of responsibility for the social issues we face is indisputable. In designing our man-made world, designers have contributed to design our problems too. Designers have helped creating the cars of people's dreams and now they have to design us right out of those cars to save us from environmental destruction.*[37]

---

[37]N. Tromp and P. Hekkert. 2018. *Designing for Society: Products and Services for a Better World* (London, UK: Bloomsbury).

Design has played a role in the softer issues of our times even if mundane designs such as buildings, cars, and smartphones may have created and heightened intercultural tension. Organizations and citizens now understand better that our physical and virtual environments affect our social interactions, management culture, and society at large.

All this reveals a paradox of contemporary design leadership: on the one hand, designers spread our design thinking methodologies to those who fight social issues, whereas on the other they continue to design our society in ways that actually sustain these same social issues. It would clearly be more efficient if organizations and design management at large could better anticipate the social implications of their design outputs. This might be the best opportunity ever to broaden the influence of design thinking, design management, and design: a coherent and coordinated, design-driven effort toward improving society at large. Which direction design takes next remains to be seen. The discussion seems to continue, and new models, terms, and dogmas are introduced at the same speed as before. In the meantime – and irrespective of this discussion – many design students are still trained to design as if nothing had happened, whereas more and more progressive design schools and professors, as well as more and more business schools, gradually integrate the constantly changing and most recent takes on design thinking into their curricula. In the years to come, this will inevitably change design practice, as well as the landscape surrounding design and designers. One specific development, however, might prove to be the ultimate turning point for bridging design and business: service design.

PART 7

It seems like service design has the potential to play a bridging role between design and business, or, quite possibly, be the bridge between the two.

Service Design: A Bridge to Cross

As referred to at the very beginning of this book, over the last two decades, service design has conquered a significant role where design is being discussed – in part as the economy at large has become increasingly dependent on services, as opposed to tangible products, and in part as the nature of transactions has shifted from taking place primarily in physical environments to depending almost entirely on digital interactions. Service design – as all other design disciplines – has been subjected to a variety of definitions and narratives, most of them quite complex in their own right. One highly condensed way of framing the core of service design could be "to facilitate, through design thinking, a transaction or exchange between a supplier and the user of a service."[1]

As private and public sectors alike recognize the importance of "facilitating transactions" to cut costs, enhance effectiveness and productivity, and exploit the potential of new technologies, service design has been able to capture the attention of business leaders and leaders within public organizations to a degree, which is quite remarkable compared with their prior interest in the "old" design disciplines. In fact, it seems like service design has the potential to play a bridging role between design and business, or quite possibly be the bridge between the two.

One of the reasons why service design appears to resonate much more easily with business leaders than design as such might be that it feels

[1]T. Edwards (ed.). 2016. "Service Design," *The Bloomsbury Encyclopedia of Design* 3, p. 213.

closer to home. Service design is not so much about forms and shapes and materials, all belonging to a universe quite distant from the daily boardroom discussions. Being all about "transactions or exchanges," service design is about customer service and experience, about smoothness and efficiency, and about doing things smarter than before, all of which have always been discussed in the C-suite. Moreover, "when we measure service performance in the right way, we can prove that service design results in more effective employment of resources, human, capital and natural."[2] Moreover, the effects of service design are often much easier to measure, as it merely requires a before-and-after approach to see the results. And, as the lack of metrics and reliable measures for the effect of design has always been a barrier to design adoption, service design might be the mediator many have missed. The need for business leaders to engage in the design process of enhanced services or business models also seems more obvious:

> *It may be argued that designing successful, holistic services needs to be approached in an integrated, multi-disciplinary way that includes most design disciplines in addition to visionary leadership.*[3]

Service design as a bridge does not only connect business thinking and practice to service design as a field on its own, but absorbs several different design approaches, methodologies, and techniques. Hence, the bridge could potentially connect business to design – at large.

> *Service design as a perspective relies on the understanding of service as value creation, where distinctions between tangibles and intangibles are beside the point. Instead, the design focus is transferred to complex relations, interactions and actors. However, the implementation of a service logic demands explicit knowledge of how to develop and design*

---

[2] A. Polaine, L. LØvlie and B. Reeson. 2013. *Service Design: From Insight to Inspiration* (New York, NY: Rosenfeld Media).

[3] J. Gloppen. *Service Design Leadership* [DeThinkingService – ReThinkingDesign, First Nordic Conference on Service Design and Service Innovation]. Oslo; November 24th-26th, 2009.

products, communication, interactions, and so on, which all together form the intended context for value creation. Then service design becomes an approach for how to organize these different design practices with the aim of contributing to the value creation as such, and as an integration of tangible and intangible design objects.[4]

Services are growing. Not only as a business domain as opposed to products, but increasingly as an integrated part of complex business strategies, encompassing both – as well as existing both physically and in digital environments. An example could be the shift that global supplier of home products IKEA is foreseeing from producing and selling furniture to becoming a service provider through leasing furniture to consumers:

IKEA will test furniture leasing in 30 markets during 2020– . . . to support customers to acquire, care for and pass on IKEA products in more sustainable ways. This is a response to consumer research exploring how to meet customers' needs in ways that contribute to a circular economy.[5]

Such a shift is not without implications. It requires the design of an entirely new value chain, new stories, new mechanisms for delivery, collection, and redelivery – just to mention a few. However, they are not internal business processes that can be optimized through process reengineering. They all involve customers and rely on their experience – from touchpoint to touchpoint – of being as good as they always expected from IKEA. This is business development that requires exactly what Katarina Edman describes as "explicit knowledge of how to develop and design products, communication, interactions, and so on, which all together form the intended context for value creation." Business leaders recognize this, and there's only one place to look: toward service design – just across the bridge from where they stand. By embracing service design as a relevant means of business development, the chances are quite overwhelming

---

[4] K.W. Edman. *Service Design: A Conceptualization of an Emerging Practice* [Thesis for the degree of Licentiate of Philosophy in Design, Faculty of Fine, Applied and Performing Arts]. Gothenburg, Sweden: University of Gothenburg; 2011.

[5] www.ikea.com

that business leaders also encounter and see the value of some of the individual components of service design – and, as it were, of design at its core. One of those is codesigning:

> *Codesign allows a design team to combine two sets of knowledge that are key to service design: Customer insights into latent user needs and in-house professionals' conversion of promising new ideas into viable concepts.* [6]

Other typical design tools and approaches, which will inevitably also grow on business leaders as they come to value service design as a means of business development are prototyping and visualizations of ideas, adjusting to feedback and prototyping again, as a cyclic path toward good user experiences, working with scenarios and narratives, and the constant dialogue with various stakeholders as the process progresses. Seeing that service design processes cannot be managed with the same background and tools as many other business processes, this, in turn, might open some managers' eyes to the specificities of design practice and design professionals. All because design, after 70 years of struggling against windmills, has finally hit a note that resonates with the business community. The meeting can now start…

As Anna Valtonen described masterly 15 years ago,

> *As the amount of designers has grown, also the potential working positions thereof have grown. … In every decade the designers have actively strived to participate in the development process in an earlier stage, and also to increase their own impact on this process and business in general.*[7]

---

[6] J. Trischler, S. Pervan, S.J. Kelly and D.R. Scott. 2018. "The Value of Codesign: The Effect of Customer Involvement in Service Design Teams," *Journal of Service Research* 21, no. 1, pp. 75-100.

[7] A. Valtonen. 2005. *Six Decades and Six Different Roles for the Industrial Designer* [Nordes Conference in the Making]. Copenhagen; May 30-31, 2005.

Based on Valtonen's studies, this role has evolved from being ***the creator*** in the fifties, via the role of being ***a creative*** – however anonymous and diplomatic team player for the industry in the sixties, an end-user expert with ergonomics and usability as the main focus in the seventies, a coordinator of brand values and appearance in the eighties, a warrantor of coherent user experiences in the nineties, and a driver of innovation at the very beginning of the new millennium. During the last decade, the role of designers and design has focused on covering new grounds and at the same time fighting to maintain an autonomous identity as a professional field. Certain design disciplines became commoditized and ended up as subdeliveries to global consultancy firms, whereas others remained anecdotal as they always were. Service design found its own professional identity and somehow managed to attract the attention of both private and public sector service providers – better than any other design discipline before them. Perhaps the role of service design will be to act as a bridge to the business community, whereas the rest of the design sector focuses on convincing that not only service design, but also professional designers across disciplines, deliver measurable value for suppliers of products, services, and user experiences. Just as they always did, but as they needed service design to help them communicate and persuade.

The increasing role and space that design has captured across sectors over the last couple of decades is incontestable, and there is no immediate reason to believe that this role will be diminished in the years to come. Service design has been very efficient in popularizing design methods. Many of its key components, such as stakeholder engagement and collaborative creative processes – from workshops to hackathons and design sprints, working with scenarios, prototyping and visual narratives, and striving for solutions that make the most possible sense, exploiting both technological and natural resources to their fullest, and leaving the least possible footprint – will remain part of responsible development of products, services, and systems.

New books on design methods are flooding the market, and there is now no such thing as a creative black design box anymore. Design methods are material artefacts and are used as intermediary objects in all kinds of design projects by designers across disciplines. And, at the end of the day, a shift toward customer centricity is what we aim for, regardless of whether the approach is service design, web design, experience design, or UX design. The idea of user centricity is easy to grasp by anyone. Moreover, service design could be the point of departure for a cultural shift where the customer is always at the heart of your business and your corporate culture. It is an effective approach to understand design as a management tool and a tool to reinvent the organization itself, from human-centered design to human-centered management – or humanistic capitalism. Who wins the battle for ownership of these components is an open question, but there is no doubt that the interest in design thinking and design management – though not always with the same degree of consciousness – shown by the management consulting community and business schools of this world indicates that these components may possibly be hard to hold on to for what we know today as the professional design community. What we might also see, however, is that some of the other and more subtle components of design as we know it – the quest for aesthetic resonance and wow factor, the form-follows-function regime, user advocacy, user-centeredness and usability, and the effect of celebrity and iconicity – may either suffer from a similar degree of domain rivalry to the one that we've seen for design methods and processes or, adversely, stand more clear-cut and crisper than ever, thus reinventing or reinvigorating design as a craft and professional practice, as a domain of intrinsic and indisputable value, as well as of constantly expanding relevance. Anyhow, there is a battle being fought out there, however subtly:

> *...the search for opportunities to innovate is everybody's job, so everybody designs ... Design thinking is seen as a problem-solving process appropriate for use by a wide variety of people. Design tools like jobs to be done, journey mapping, visualization and prototyping become as much a part of the manager's tool kit as Excel spreadsheets, as much a part of a teacher's tool kit as lesson plans and as much a part of a nurse's tool kit as a stethoscope.*[8]

---

[8] J. Liedtka, R. Salzman and D. Azer. 2017. *Design Thinking for the Greater Good Innovation in the Social Sector* (Columbia: Columbia Business School Publishing).

Service Design for Redesign of a Territory: A Story from Real Life

To challenge our own thinking, we interviewed Diana Arsovic Nielsen, who trained as an architect, and who is currently Director of Regional Development at the Capital Region of Denmark, taking as a point of departure the following questions:

- *How did you arrive at being convinced of the potential and powers of design as a strategic factor?*
- *How did you overcome the barriers of skepticism and resistance from your organization?*
- *Which particular results would you bring out as examples of how design excellence made a measurable difference?*
- *What roles do design, design thinking, and design management play in your constant striving for better performance and better results?*

Our conversation led to the following story from real life: as an integrative conceptual framework for design innovation in society.

On Skills and Competences

As an architect and designer, my own training revolved around methods, processes, and projects – not on specific topics or on building a theoretical language, or on in-depth academic analysis. And even though I always saw my own future role as a leader of a sort, I found it difficult to merge my own interest in management and leadership with what I experienced as design practice. Hence, I decided to supplement my Royal Academy of Arts studies with courses at the Copenhagen Business School, where I benefited from meeting and working closely with a wide range of students from various academic fields, who shared my interest and dilemma.

I realized that I was not truly conscious of what a designer does until I started applying my methods and processes on joint projects, which were not design projects as such. However, I turned them into design projects by focusing not so much on the end result but on how to differentiate good ideas from bad ones and how to find the right approaches and the best possible solutions to the right possible questions. That's where I started realizing how powerful design can be. While the others applied their theoretical knowledge within business intelligence, risk assessments, finance, or marketing, my methodology was the only one capturing the situation as a whole and bridging all the others' expertise. On the other hand, while they quite easily could articulate exactly what their expertise was, I had to demonstrate it through the way that I worked and by being much more hands-on in my approach to our joint projects than they were, and while they were absolutely content with a delivery consisting of a written report, I was much more focused on delivering tangible outcomes. And all this was decades before the revival of design thinking as a commonplace term.

In the real world, designers work in teams with people and in projects, where a fundamental understanding of the underlying business case is crucial, which is not at all something you learn at the academy of art. Often, I was at a loss for a language to qualify my solutions from a cost and benefit point of view – despite being brought up in a home of entrepreneurs – and understood quite early that whatever you do, there is always a "client" at the other end – someone who is willing to pay for what I do. Hence, I soon realized that I had done the right thing by adding a business school degree in management and organizational theory to my design degree. This combination of being trained at both design and management also explains why I've been on a somewhat organic journey from acting as a designer in a management-dominated environment to being part of management myself. At the same time, it's pretty obvious that I bring something different to the boardroom than my colleagues – a different mindset, a different toolbox, and, basically, just another approach to what we do, why we do it, and how we go about it. When I meet with a management team, my creative outset means that I automatically look at the situation from a different angle and ask different questions than my colleagues, often opening new avenues of exploration. At the same time, I also bring in a system for how to generate and process valuable ideas, and instead of just being duped by brilliant ideas, I pursue it with questions with regard to how it could possibly be realized and which intermediary steps – opportunities as well as barriers – are needed to get to that point; all based on my hands-on experience with countless projects, as opposed to the others and their often confined and theoretical knowledge.

What I may not be as good as them at is foreseeing bureaucratic and external factors, which could influence the project, as my starting point will always be to understand the users and what consequences any given development might have for them, and to extrapolate how other stakeholders than those, that we think of as core users, might experience it. Simply as a result of my inability to relate to an idea without also envisaging it as a service, a transaction, or a solution of a kind – digital or analogue. That's, I guess, what I was actually trained to be able to do; to extrapolate and foresee; that, at the end of the day, is the core of design methodology. My combination of design and management has also – quite naturally – attracted me to and made me an interesting candidate for managerial positions within the innovation and development domain. I don't think that I could ever have succeeded as a COO or CFO; I need to work with creative processes to deliver true value.

On Embedding Design in Organizations

Has it been difficult? Yes – and no. All people working with change and innovation face a certain degree of skepticism, thus building a language and arguments for what one does to be part of the journey. I have always invested some of my creative energy in making sure that others could see what I was doing and that the change I argued for was a change for the better. And, also, that if the change is only incremental and marginal, we haven't exploited our own innovation potential. I also learned that you need to understand the reality that you want to change. If you do not understand the tone of voice of an organization, and the way it functions, you cannot engage people in your project. If you don't – and sit there in a corner with all your fancy tools and your buzzwords and your multicolored Post-its, it's like being the captain of a ship where no one wants to be passengers. So, learning the language, the processes, and the name of the game – including financial and organizational factors – has been one of the most important preconditions for working with and understanding the context that I wanted to change, and as such there is no difference between the private and the public sectors. What can also play an important role is size. I have primarily worked in large organizations, with between 20,000 and 45,000 people, and I think that embedding design in such organizations depends on one's methods and achievements growing slowly from the inside, a little like a Trojan horse.

If you want to move people, you need to meet them on their own home turf, and if you want them to follow you, you need to understand what's at stake for them, and not for you as a designer. For some creative people, the problem is that for them the future stands crystal clear, something that may come across as witchcraft or hot air to other people; sometimes as a little ridiculous and sometimes as an outright opportunity to dismiss the work and role of the designer. Hence, it might sometimes be a good idea for designers to turn down the volume of their vision for the future and instead make sure that they create an atmosphere where looking into the future is OK and where the users can build a language and a vision together.

In one of the organizations I worked, as soon as I entered, I could see tons of opportunities for developments that would resonate globally. That, however, did not necessarily mean that all the others could see the same thing. They thought I was mad, even though now, less than a decade later, we see it happening. I'm not saying that designers are all clairvoyants, but even if they may have the ability to imagine the future, they have to respect that others might not be as visionary as they are. As such, it is also important to understand that communication is an essential element in design leadership, to make sure that design is firmly embedded in and adopted by an organization.

On Design and Design Leadership

Another essential element is to understand that it is not enough to depend on one's own professional skills and tools and to embrace one's dependence on other professionals. A good designer might have what it takes to engage others and facilitate processes, but he or she very rarely creates anything at all on his or her own. Good results – good design – come out of collaboration, and good design management is very much about making such processes as effective and as enjoyable as possible. One factor that plays a vital role to exploit an organization's creative potential is diversity. When I look at many management teams – perhaps, in particular, in the public sector, all members resemble each other and those who recruited them. It is natural and often quite unconscious, but one often hires people with skills and tools that one understands. I, on the other hand, am extremely curious about other professional backgrounds than my own, and I rarely hire anyone that even remotely resembles myself. Admittedly, I sometimes miss to have a few more designers around the table, as they normally understand quite intuitively what it is that I mean. Now, I often feel a little alienated, surrounded by people who speak another language than my own and whose references are different. But that's how one develops: by enlarging the circle of approaches and mindsets, thus also amplifying the creative power, around the table.

On the other hand, while always striving toward cross- and multidisciplinary teams, I also experienced that by hiring nurses and carpenters and process engineers, one not only gets a wide range of different angles on running a hospital, but one also risks that the same people are so different that they are not able to lead a meaningful professional conversation. Gradually, I have found that cross- and multidisciplinary individuals are equally valuable, but easier to work with. People with two different educational backgrounds, or cultural backgrounds, are much better at changing their mindsets, at understanding different languages, and at seeing things from different angles. Hence, we need to encourage leaders to hire faceted people and to look at their entire career and background, not only to what kind of job they're in right now. As a designer, one often discusses with oneself, while – as a design leader or design thinker – one accepts that the creative force does not lie within oneself, but in the team and in the interplay and in the joint journey. That's where value is created. The most difficult, though, might be to regard the ideas and input provided by others as just as genial as one's own. Not all designers are able to do so; hence they might be brilliant designers, but they will never make great design leaders.

On Prototyping and Bodily Intelligence

Having worked at an architectural studio, I had already designed a ton of different rooms and furnished them with all that makes an environment. Moving to the public sector, I got my first real understanding of how design can be done in a more meaningful manner, orchestrating a user engagement process to design the hospital ward of the future, engaging patients, staff, family members, and suppliers. We developed a 1:1 prototype, enabling fast build-up of complete environments by moving furniture and machinery and what have you around. That was the first time that I realized how powerful prototyping is to understand different concerns and priorities, different workflows, and different interests. What I saw with my own eyes with regard to how a room is conceived differently by different user groups was mind-blowing after years of studio work. The patients and families wanted comfortable and nice-looking rooms, reminding them of their homes. The medical staff prioritized ergonomics and convenience for them. The cleaning staff preferred no-fuss clinical environments without nooks and crannies, where dirt could pile. And the technical staff wanted something that was easy to build and elements that could easily be replaced. But, by everyone seeing and understanding the motives of the other groups, empathy between them was created, and a compromise that everyone could live with could actually be reached. Twenty per cent of the original floor and furnishing plans were redone after the process.

Prototyping is one of the keys to design thinking. In the boardroom and the executive offices, decisions are made on the basis of words on paper – sometimes graphs or drawings, but entirely based on our theoretical and intellectual understanding of the available information, entirely based upon what we have inside our heads. What is far too often forgotten is that the knowledge that really influences on people's lives is the knowledge that is embedded in our bodies. Prototyping is all about activating our bodily intelligence and an opportunity to see how decisions will affect people in real life, and not only expressed in data. In many ways, my mission has been to activate and exploit the intelligence which exists in the body and bodies of the organization – both the individual bodily intelligence and the knowledge represented by the organizational body, the operational parts of an organization, as opposed to the head – the management. And how does that bodily knowledge translate to something that the head will understand? Bodily experiences are not easily captured in words; so often, showing the management video captions of prototyping sessions can be much more convincing and contribute to creating a degree of professional empathy for citizens or customers or staff, or simply just a better understanding of the real-life consequences of any given decision made by the head. And despite certain biases toward being "manipulated" by having to witness real-life prototypes, it works. I've seen how it has changed public sector managers' understanding of the complexity of situations, hence also of the nuances and understanding of the business case on which their decisions were made, and ultimately also the actual decision.

Designers have often a very tangible and physical understanding of the problem that they address and the solution that they work on. To embed the same degree of understanding in the rest of the value chain, design management is needed. Most needs and problems, services and transactions can be prototyped through simple props and role play, including decision-making processes and contract negotiations. From the day we are born, we build our understanding of the world through our bodies, and to me, a fundamental assumption in and for design thinking is the recognition of the power of the knowledge and intelligence embedded in our bodies.

On User Centricity

Starting with the user in itself does not necessarily solve all problems. User centricity also requires a certain shopping around for knowledge to complete the picture, and the wider the range of sources, the more complete your pool of available knowledge becomes. Moreover, the different ways of user engagement need to be properly dosed, depending on which knowledge you seek and how you intend to use it. If you want to understand someone's problem, observing might be more effective than asking, and if you want to know whether a certain solution will be accepted or not, asking user groups to test it might be more appropriate than asking what they think. It all depends on which output you need to improve on the solution. Often, user engagement is being used uncritically and by inviting a bunch of people on a field trip with role play and refreshments. Which can be fine, if it is also the most effective way of doing it, but on the other hand, it does not guarantee the quality of the information one can gather. The key is to use professional facilitators to get the information one needs, engage the right people at the right time in the process and in the most effective way. Innovation is a craft, and so is facilitation – and the craft needs to be of the highest quality. Likewise, both innovation and facilitation take practice, and there is no rule saying that just because you're a good designer, you're also a good facilitator.

My own driving force is to develop services of such value to the citizens that they are willing to cofinance their existence, which requires that you start with and seriously and professionally engage them as appropriate throughout the process. If, however, an organization internalizes this fundamental assumption – that "we are here for them, not the other way around" – it will influence on all our decision-making processes and on how we all perceive our role as service providers, including the fact that the day you do not any longer deliver value to your users, your "business" will slowly die. What design can, furthermore, do is not necessarily break down, but at least compensate for the existence of silos by creating a common understanding of who, at the other end of the silos, it is that we work for. Design can visualize the value that needs to be created, hence also what the best possible solution could be. By starting a project upon a joint understanding of a project's objective, one also ensures that what takes place within each one of the silos supports the overall goal instead of super-optimization of the interests of the individual silo.

On Design, Design Management, and Design Thinking

One might ask which competences we need to foster cocreation. Throughout the academic world, we nurture narrow and specialized knowledge – profound professional excellence. What we are getting more and more aware of is that to benefit from such excellence, we also need the facilities, tools, and competences to reach out to and create value across all kinds of expertise. Unfortunately, as long as we continue building our academic excellence on a bachelor, where basic building blocks are laid down, and a master, where we specialize within a corner of our field, sometimes followed by a postgraduate degree with an even narrower focus, we actually miss out on building the competences needed to build academic bridges. Hence, those who are in the best place to further develop their skills to do so are designers and architects, but they cannot do it all on their own. We also need people with other backgrounds, who are curious of and fascinated by the cross-disciplinary. Design can be narrow or open, but helps materialize and understand what can be, but which doesn't yet exist. It is about making ideas tangible by creating prototypes and visual representations to help people understand and relate to possible solutions, and a core value in design is still, and has to be, how to make solutions attractive and desirable. Design management – and innovation management – is all about building and organizing relations between different skills and expertise in an organization that can contribute to better solutions – and about aligning what we often refer to as design processes with strategic goals. And design thinking is all about how to create a common understanding of the tools and to grant an organization the resources needed for design and design management to contribute to better results.

And the wonderful thing is that design and innovation – and all related terms and concepts – are and have to be subject to constant change. If they weren't, none of them would either have or deserve any credibility whatsoever.

PART 8

Design can successfully address the challenges faced by business leaders across the world – challenges such as innovation, human capital, digital and technological capabilities, competitive advantage, and customer experience. However, the entire value chain needs to work. At the same time, the value created on all three levels, operational, functional, and strategic, needs to be acknowledged in its own right.

Final Reflections from the Authors

Having accepted the reality that continuous change is here to stay, one might still ask where all this is heading? What role will design play, and what will be the most significant changes to design practice, design management, and design thinking in the next decade or two...? In the absence of a crystal ball, the following cannot be any other than predictions and qualified guesses. The role of design has never evolved in isolation but as a mirror of business model, organizational and technological innovation, of changes in social structures and behavior, and of all other developments taking place alongside its own evolution. Hence, the perception of what design is and its place and role in business and society changes accordingly.

Design is increasingly recognized for creating value in the intersections of society and social challenges, sustainability (environment, social, economic), and the circular economy; the oncoming global challenges have an interdisciplinary nature, and design has the potential to create value in multiple intersections. At the same time, the very concept of value is changing. What was seen earlier as a simple profit/loss equation is now recognized as a complex construction where value is created and consumed in novel ways and where well-being co-exists happily with profit, and eco-footprint is[1]

The future role of design and designers has been a recurring theme of design thinkers and opinion leaders, and a bountiful basket of foresights have been published for decades already.

Design has moved out of the domain in which a delivery is most often a tangible answer to a brief and into a domain, where design is seen as a valid resource where large, complex challenges are at stake, increasingly linked to customer experience, and where the designer works in close and equivalent collaboration with all kinds of other professional disciplines. Such challenges could be efficiency or profitability related – most probably on long term, or it could be related to local, regional or national identity or external relations, to loyalty issues and internal relations in large corporations, to competitiveness and innovation capacity, democratic processes and engagement, cross–sectorial dialogue and diversity issues. Not to forget the probably most urgent of all challenges: the need for a more sustainable corporate and political development and for a more responsible and balanced global order.[2]

A New Generation of Leaders and Decision Makers

One doesn't need to be a notorious dystopian to predict that the coming generations face some quite unnerving challenges, of which we already see the contours: *extreme weather events, large-scale involuntary migration, major natural disasters, large-scale terrorist attacks, massive incidents of data fraud or theft, weapons of mass destruction, water crises, and failure*

[1]L. Svengren Holm, M. Koria, B. Jevnaker and A. Rieple. 2017. Introduction: Design creating value at intersections. *Proceedings from Design Management Academy Conference*, pp. 157-60, Hong Kong.

[2]P. GrØnbech and S. Valade-Amland (ed.). 2010. "Manifesto." In *The Role of Design in the 21st Century*. Copenhagen: Danish Designers.

of climate,[3] the challenges discussed in an earlier chapter, as identified by CEOs in a global PwC survey. How will we deal with these challenges in the future? A publication by Harvard Kennedy School, addressing how we face global challenges, sums it up quite precisely:

> *A special form of leadership, system leadership, is needed to tackle global challenges like food security, climate change, job creation, and gender parity. These challenges are complex and systemic, rooted in the actions and interactions of diverse yet interconnected, interdependent stakeholders. Leaders in business, government, and civil society increasingly recognize that they cannot be addressed in a top-down, pre-planned, linear fashion and that point solutions don't work. Instead, the solutions require stakeholders to change the way they operate at the global, national, and local levels. Over time, they must develop new technologies, products, services, business models, public service delivery models, policy and regulatory innovations, voluntary standards, and cultural norms and behaviors that together deliver new results.*[4]

One thing that the future might bring – more widespread than today – is the emergence of the DEO – design executive officer. Giudice and Ireland even claim that "[p]utting a traditional CEO in front of a modern workforce is anachronistic" – and they explain why:

> *DEO, Design Executive Officers, possess behaviors and mindsets that enable them to excel in unpredictable, fast moving conditions. They help nurture and retain talented employees. They lead teams who learn from one another and collaborate easily and effectively. Business acumen and creative ability are not siloed anymore. Every business challenge is a design problem solvable with imagination and metrics.*[5]

---

[3]World Economic Forum 2007-2017, *Global Risks Reports (Agglomeration of Top 5 Global Risks in terms of Likelihood/Impact).*

[4]J. Nelson and B. Jenkins. 2016. Tackling Global Challenges. *Lessons in System Leadership from the World Economic Forum's New Vision for Agriculture Initiative,* CSR Initiative at the Harvard Kennedy School.

[5]M. Giudice and C. Ireland. 2013. *The rise of the DEO Leadership by Design* (San Francisco, CA: New Riders Publishing, Pearson).

Leaders as System Thinkers

Peter Senge has been an advocate of system thinking for people in business leadership – an idea that has been omnipresent when writing this book: to take an integrative approach to design, design management, and design thinking, with no boundaries. To play a role in tomorrow's regenerative economy, we have to learn to see the larger system, including its natural and societal limits.

> *Design plays a central role in shaping a sustainable civilization. It does so in the material dimension of product design, architecture, industrial design and town and regional planning as well as in the immaterial dimension of the meta design of concepts and inclusive multi perspectives from which a holistic/integral worldview can emerge.*[6]

Why Matter Matters

We started this book by advocating that ***theory matters*** as a bridging tool. We end by insisting on matter. ***Matter matters.*** Whether through products, services, spaces, documents, digital apps, bodies, processes, seeing the beauty in them is system thinking. Designers – or those who learn from them – are able to think in metaphors. Materiality in organizations helps to explore connections and networks, and as we gradually exceed the biological limitations of our present brain, we need new meta skills that can only come from doing.

> *There are five talents, the meta skills that I believe will serve us best in the future in an age of non-stop innovation: feeling, seeing, dreaming, making, learning.... The bright thread that weaves all five meta skills is aesthetics, a set of sensory-based principles that can stitch together the new and the beautiful.*[7]

---

[6]D.C. Wahl. 2016. *Designing Regenerative Cultures* (London, UK: Triarchy Press).

[7]M. Neumeier. 2013. *Meta Skills; Five Talents for the Robotic Age* (San Francisco, CA: New Rider, Pearson).

That's a reassuring endnote, if any. Yet it emphasizes the need for a systemic approach also to design, engaging stakeholders and exploiting untapped potential – of designers, of managers, and business leaders – and of building bridges between, instead of silos around, them. Design, design management, and design thinking form a value chain on its own in this landscape, regardless of whether the objective is to address systemic challenges and what the design theorist Horst Rittel named ***wicked problems***[8] as they occur:

> *The problem for designers is to conceive and plan what does not yet exist, and this occurs in the context of the indeterminacy of wicked problems, before the final result is known.*[9]

Or, to successfully address the challenges faced by business leaders across the world, challenges such as innovation, human capital, digital and technological capabilities, competitive advantage, and customer experience,[10] the entire value chain needs to work. At the same time, the value created on all three levels – operational, functional, and strategic – needs to be acknowledged in its own right. If they work in harmony, through the empowerment to work systemically and strategically with design through aspirational and inspirational leadership, through the allocation of management structures and resources to enable the inclusive and explorative processes needed, and through attracting the competences needed to embody the most innovative, responsible and attractive solutions possible, design is potentially one of the most powerful instruments of change there is. Not instead of or to contest the invaluable legacy of management thinking that already exist, based on decades of studies by gurus like Kim & Mauborgne, Hamel & Prahalad, Christensen, Chesbrough, Pine & Gilmore, Porter, Argyris,

---

[8]W. Churchman. December 1967. "Wicked Problem," *Management Science* 14, no. 4.

[9]R. Buchanan. October 1990. *Wicked Problems in Design Thinking*. Paper presented at 'Colloque Recherches sur le Design: Incitations, Implications, Interactions', Vol. VIII, no. 2, Spring 1992.

[10]PwC. 2017. *20th CEO Survey: 20 Years Inside the Mind of the CEO... What's Next?* (London, UK: PwC), p. 12.

Nonaka & Takeuchi, Mintzberg, or Weick, or any other of the highly respected scholars referred to in this book.

> ***We have merely tried to build a bridge between research and consultancy, between design science and business science, theory, and practice.***

With due respect for their complementary worldview and the complementary talents they produce. And with a strong belief that the future calls for decision makers who understand that matter matters and who believe in the primacy of purpose.

About the Authors

Brigitte Borja de Mozota After 10 years of working in business with designers, she started in a new career in academia at Paris University. She received her PhD in economics at Université Paris I Sorbonne in 1985. Pioneer in the field of design management from a business science viewpoint, she was key to the creation of its scientific territory through international networks and conferences worldwide: Design Management Institute 1988, European Academy of Research 1993, Ateliers de la Recherche en Design 2006, and design research journals (*Design Journal*, *Sciences du Design*) and research laboratories.

In addition to publishing a wealth of research papers and studies, she is the author of the reference book *Design Management – Using Design to Build Brand Value and Corporate Innovation*, published in France in 1990 and republished in 2002, and in English, in 2003, by Allworth Press, New York, and translated into Turkish in 2005; Korean and Italian in 2008; Spanish, Brazilian, Farsi and Japanese in 2010; and Chinese in 2011. She is Life Fellow of the Design Management Institute (Boston), www.dmi.org.

She has supervised PhD candidates and trained master's students, in both business and design schools, in design and innovation and is considered an authority on design economics in France.

Currently a consultant as well as professor and supervisor of MBA "Managing by design" theses, she concentrates on mission-driven projects that offer tools to a larger public to help in understanding the value of the design industry and innovation and leadership challenges in economics.

Recent work concerns the KCDM center with Slovenian companies and research on topics like designers' "soft skills" as strategic meta skills required in the digital age, design in supply chain, and UX design and agile transformation (linkedin.com/in/brigitte-borja-de-mozota-7391126)

Steinar Valade-Amland After holding export, product, and marketing management positions in the private sector— primarily in design-based manufacturing companies, he worked as account director and CEO of a leading brand design agency in Copenhagen from 1997 to 2000, and then as managing director of the Association of Danish Designers until 2012. Since then, he has acted as an independent consultant through his own set-up, THREE POINT ZERO, working for companies in industries as diverse as pharmaceuticals, lifestyle products, and tourism, as well as Danish and international NGOs and public sector organizations. Currently, he works mostly with the creative industries, including as head of strategy and business development in a design consultancy serving the global market. He is frequently consulted for his expertise in matters related to design and innovation processes and methodology, among others as evaluator of research and innovation initiatives, supported by the European Union. He has held numerous honorary positions and has frequently been invited to deliver keynote addresses and has served as guest lecturer and as panelist; in addition, he has contributed to several books, including *Creative Sprint,* published by the University of Brandenburg in 2014, presented 15 entries to the *Bloomsbury Encyclopedia of Design* in 2015, and written numerous articles in trade magazines. He is the author of the peer-reviewed book *INNOLITERACY – From Design Thinking to Tangible Change*, published in Danish, in 2016, and in English by Business Expert Press, in 2018 (linkedin.com/in/steinarvaladeamland).

Index

OTHER TITLES IN OUR PORTFOLIO AND PROJECT MANAGEMENT COLLECTION

Timothy Kloppenborg, *Editor*

- *Discoveries Through Personal Agility* by Raji Sivaraman and Michal Raczka
- *Project Communications: A Critical Factor for Project Success* by Connie Plowman and Jill Diffendal
- *Quantitative Tools of Project Management* by David L. Olson
- *The People Project Triangle: Balancing Delivery, Business-as-Usual, and People's Welfare* by Stuart Copeland and Andy Coaton
- *How to Fail at Change Management: A Manager's Guide to the Pitfalls of Managing Change* by James Marion and John Lewis
- *Core Concepts of Project Management* by David L. Olson
- *Projects, Programs, and Portfolios in Strategic Organizational Transformation* by James Jiang and Gary Klein
- *Capital Project Management, Volume III: Evolutionary Forces* by Robert N. McGrath
- *Capital Project Management, Volume II: Capital Project Finance* by Robert N. McGrath
- *Capital Project Management, Volume I: Capital Project Strategy* by Robert N. McGrath
- *Executing Global Projects: A Practical Guide to Applying the PMBOK Framework in the Global Environment* by James Marion and Tracey Richardson
- *Project Communication from Start to Finish: The Dynamics of Organizational Success* by Geraldine E. Hynes
- *The Lost Art of Planning Projects* by Louise Worsley and Christopher Worsley
- *Project Portfolio Management, Second Edition: A Model for Improved Decision Making* by Clive N. Enoch
- *Adaptive Project Planning* by Louise Worsley and Christopher Worsley
- *Passion, Persistence, and Patience: Key Skills for Achieving Project Success* by Alfonso Bucero
- *Leveraging Business Analysis for Project Success, Second Edition* by Vicki James
- *Project Management Essentials, Second Edition* by Kathryn N. Wells and Timothy J. Kloppenborg
- *Agile Working and the Digital Workspace: Best Practices for Designing and Implementing Productivity* by John Eary